ANTONI
LET'S DO
DINNER

ANTONI
LET'S DO
DINNER

ANTONI POROWSKI

with Mindy Fox

Photographs by Paul Brissman

HOUGHTON MIFFLIN HARCOURT   BOSTON   NEW YORK   2021

Copyright © 2021 by Speedy Popo, LLC

Photographs © 2021 by Paul Brissman

All rights reserved

For information about permission to reproduce selections from this book, write to trade.permissions@hmhco.com or to Permissions, Houghton Mifflin Harcourt Publishing Company, 3 Park Avenue, 19th Floor, New York, New York 10016.

hmhbooks.com

Book design and hand lettering by Laura Palese

Food styling by Maggie Ruggiero and Lisa Homa

Prop styling by Kristine Trevino

Library of Congress Cataloging-in-Publication Data is available.

ISBN 978-0-358-39532-4 (hbk)

ISBN 978-0-358-46628-4 (signed ed)

ISBN 978-0-358-47128-8 (signed ed)

Printed in the United States

1 2021

4500828873

To LP,
Thank you for
giving me the
courage to grow
from my fears.

Thank-Yous

The only thing more shocking than writing my first-ever acknowledgments for my first-ever cookbook is getting to do it a second time around. When my first cookbock was published, a dear, wise friend asked me how it felt to have a book out in the world for people to read and cook from. To my self-deprecating reply, she responded, "There is no shame in being proud of your work. You are allowed to be excited, you know." I am indeed very proud. It took the trust and help of many people to create this new collection of recipes.

My appreciation can only start with my coauthor, MINDY FOX. You and I spent countless hours cooking side by side in New York City, as well as conferring on the phone, and your work on this book has deepened my appreciation for your endless dedication to words and recipes. Call me sentimental, but our little recipe-development team made my apartment feel like a home, and for that, I have you to thank. Every single day you taught me something new, be it the versatility of my broiler or the magic of cayenne pepper. I, in turn, gave you a stress banana, so you're welcome for that. You somehow continue to organize my chaotic mind and remind me to keep things simple yet thoughtful. Thank you for sticking around, and for being someone I can talk to for hours about grocery shopping and Kewpie mayo.

To our culinary assistant, SADIE GELB; I am so happy you were part of our project. Thank you for lugging in ingredients every morning—you always knew where to get the best shrimp, cheese, or bread, never settling for lesser options—and for teaching me how to make the perfect jammy-yolked egg. I'm sorry for immediately throwing you onto my Insta stories as soon as I realized you were a bit shy, but I'm glad I broke you in—the wealth of knowledge and precision you brought to this book helped make it what it is.

GINA GABRIEL, God help me if I had to do any of this without you. While Mindy, Sadie, and I were typing away or recipe testing, you managed the rest of my insane world so I could focus. Thank you for stepping in to help with ingredient sourcing one day, or fixing the stupid printer another. You are the queen of multitasking, able to juggle a call with Delta to change one of my flights for the fourth time while simultaneously scoring me tickets to the American Kennel Club's Meet the Breeds event. I start to get anxiety when I think about everything you manage and coordinate on a daily basis! Thank you again for doing what you do. Also a special shout out to BRIANNA KAUFMAN for keeping Ben in check and always going the extra mile.

To my editor, RUX MARTIN, I'm as happy you've kept your iconic hairstyle as I am that you were just as direct and honest with your feedback and expertise this go-around as you were with the first book. You see and articulate things so clearly, with no room for bullshit, and I love you for that. I'm sorry I dragged you out of retirement, but to be frank, no one could have done a better job.

To photographer PAUL BRISSMAN and assistant TOM WOOL, it's an honor to continue working together. Paul, they don't come better than you. Focused and unobtrusive, you're a damn ninja.

Food stylists MAGGIE RUGGIERO and LISA HOMA, and prop stylist KRISTINE TREVINO, you see the beauty and art of the way food is presented. I'm in awe of your talents. Thanks as well to assistants VERONICA MARTINEZ, TIFFANY SCHLEIGH, SARAH ABRAMS, SIMONE MANDELL, and ERIKA DUGAN.

Book designer LAURA PALESE, thank you for taking the extra step in elevating this book with hand-lettered fonts and artfully making it all so enjoyable to our eyes.

My sincere thanks to the team at HMH, especially publisher DEB BRODY, for your faith in me. Art director MELISSA LOTFY made sure the cover was both classic and distinctive. Editor SARAH KWAK expertly managed a million details. Copyeditor JUDITH SUTTON stared down errors and MARINA PADAKIS marched them right out. CRYSTAL PAQUETTE worked with the printer to make this beautiful.

Styling and glam squad **CHLOE HARTSTEIN**, **AMY KOMOROWSKI**, and **JESSICA ORTIZ**, it's not the clothing you select or de-puffing potions you apply that I love you for. It's the care you take, so I feel confident before every photo is taken that I not only look my best but feel like a champ too. I'm so grateful to work with you both.

To my friends **REEMA SAMPAT**, **GIGI HADID**, **JONATHAN VAN NESS**, and **TAN FRANCE**, thank you for bringing your beautiful mugs to the pages of this book.

To **CARRIE GORDON** at LEDE Public Relations and your dynamo team, **MATTHEW AVENTO**, **EMMA EALES**, and **KAROLINA SURAWSKI**, thank you for guiding me in every pursuit I embark on. You're all superstars.

To my family, both Polish and French Canadian: **DAD**, thank you for the daily reminder to stay humble, even when I'm bobsledding in Switzerland. I learned to communicate my love through food because that's what I saw you doing, and I wanted to be just like you. To my sis and brother-in-law, **KAROLINA** and **PIOTR**, I love you both so much. Karo, you're a warrior and you teach me strength with your very existence every day. **SYLVIE**, my rational French-Canadian mom, it's totally OK that you love Tan as much as you do me. Everyone in your life is lucky to have you. You've raised three good ones I am blessed to consider siblings. **VALERIE**, **PIERRE-OLIVIER**, and **SIMON**, I'm sorry my French accent is pretentious.

To **KEVIN**, thank you for being my best taste-tester and my compass for the things that matter most.

To my CAA literary family: My book agent, **DAVID LARABELL**, thank you for your continued guidance, support, and encouragement. **KATE CHILDS**, you elevate books into experiences for readers and fans with your publicity expertise. I look forward to more 5:00 a.m. flights together on tour, justifying our often-questionable food choices along the way.

To my best friend and agent, **BEN LEVINE**: When I think of you and all we've accomplished together in such a short amount of time, I shake my head in disbelief. Our kinship as young assistants evolved to client and agent, and while our working relationship has changed, our friendship has only grown stronger, and that is the part I care most about—but please keep getting me jobs! You have been my biggest champion.

—ANTONI POROWSKI

To dear **ANTONI**, enormous gratitude and then some. Thank you for another exciting culinary adventure together. You make work light and fun, and you're way more organized than you give yourself credit for. I couldn't wish for a more trusted friend and collaborator.

To our editor, **RUX MARTIN**; your spirited late-night text messages and savvy thinking kept us on our toes. You're simply the best.

To our culinary assistant, **SADIE GELB**; your talent, dedication, kindness, smarts, and sweet sense of humor are unmatched. Working with you is always a dream.

To **GINA GABRIEL**, thank you for your skillful scheduling, keen cross-testing, and limitless daily good vibes.

To **DAWN PERRY**, Antoni and I both thank you for terrific and calm-inducing pinch-hitting when our time narrowed at a critical deadline moment.

To my agent, **SARAH SMITH**, at David Black Agency; you make so much magic happen. I am beyond lucky to have you in my court.

I am deeply grateful to my **FOX**, **HOFFMAN**, and **RUDLEY FAMILIES**, near and far, and the many friends and colleagues who continue to cheer me on.

And to my husband, **STEVE HOFFMAN**, and our treasured canine companion, **JASPER**, your love makes everything possible.

—MINDY FOX

Contents

Welcome to Dinner

"What's my main veg?" That's the first thing I ask myself when I'm thinking about dinner. If I'm making chicken, for instance, and it's late summer or fall, I think about red onions and grapes. Then I rub the legs and thigh pieces with smoky chile powder and roast everything together on the same sheet pan, tossing in some rosemary or whatever herb I've got. As they cook, the grapes burst and mingle with the crispy chicken, sweet charred onions, and woodsy herbs—super tasty and super simple.

My dinners throughout the week tend to follow a pattern. On Monday and Tuesday, I typically stay plant-based, with white bean chili, crispy tofu on an arugula salad, or a one-pot cauliflower and chickpea curry in a gingery, creamy broth made with coconut milk. By Wednesday, though, I want something more substantial, like meatballs and eggplant, made uber-easy by that "fast cooker" hiding in plain sight: my broiler. At the tail end of the week, I lean into decadence with a skillet-seared steak luxuriously slathered with spicy butter. I pair that with a fresh parsley salad, one of the sleeper hits in this book. On other nights, I fall back on another one of my secret weapons, eggs, and make a soft scramble with shrimp and scallions.

Come Saturday and Sunday, I just want comfort. Time for my favorite nachos! I pile them high with shredded rotisserie chicken, diced tomato and onion, fresh and pickled jalapeños, canned beans, and sharp cheddar, and eat them while binge-watching reruns of *30 Rock*. Or I cook up my take on childhood: a pot of turkey cheeseburger soup, with rafts of melted cheese and pickle toast.

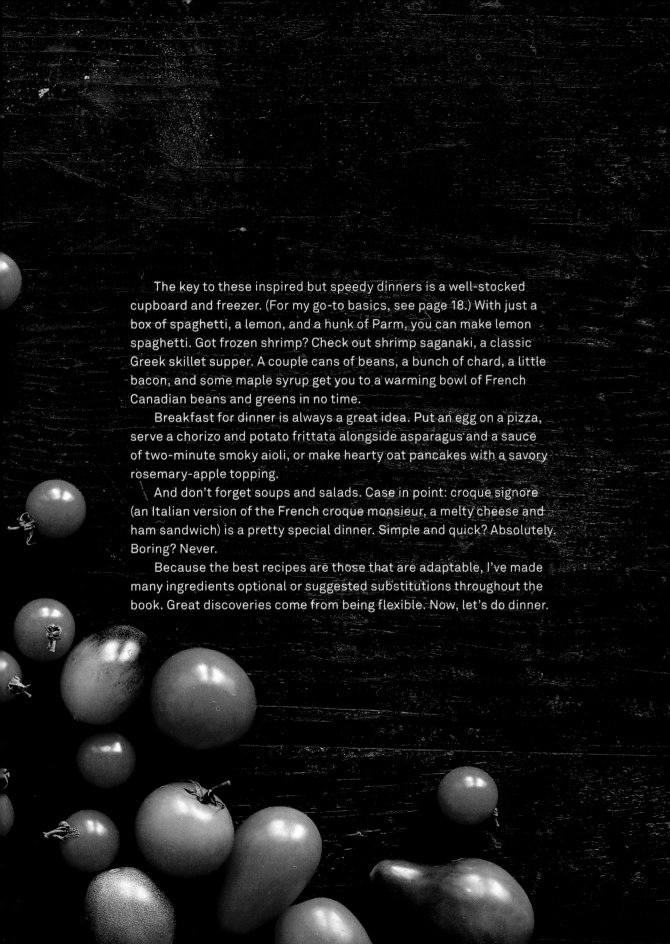

The key to these inspired but speedy dinners is a well-stocked cupboard and freezer. (For my go-to basics, see page 18.) With just a box of spaghetti, a lemon, and a hunk of Parm, you can make lemon spaghetti. Got frozen shrimp? Check out shrimp saganaki, a classic Greek skillet supper. A couple cans of beans, a bunch of chard, a little bacon, and some maple syrup get you to a warming bowl of French Canadian beans and greens in no time.

Breakfast for dinner is always a great idea. Put an egg on a pizza, serve a chorizo and potato frittata alongside asparagus and a sauce of two-minute smoky aioli, or make hearty oat pancakes with a savory rosemary-apple topping.

And don't forget soups and salads. Case in point: croque signore (an Italian version of the French croque monsieur, a melty cheese and ham sandwich) is a pretty special dinner. Simple and quick? Absolutely. Boring? Never.

Because the best recipes are those that are adaptable, I've made many ingredients optional or suggested substitutions throughout the book. Great discoveries come from being flexible. Now, let's do dinner.

10 Fast Favorites

While all the recipes in this book are about spending more time eating and less time preparing food, these are the ten dishes I turn to when I'm really in a rush.

Smoked Trout Niçoise with Lemony
Scallion Dressing, page 28

Creamy Soft-Scrambled Eggs with
Shrimp & Scallions, page 82

Masala Spinach Omelette,
page 85

French-Canadian Beans & Greens
with Brown Bread, page 237

Armenian Pita Pizza
(Lahmajoun), page 119

Lemon Spaghetti with Toasted Walnuts
& Parsley, page 130

Chicken Rice Bowl with
Chili Mayo & Ginger, page 194

Broiled Fish & Asparagus with
Choose-Your-Flavor Butter Sauce, page 172

Strip Steak with Harissa Butter
& Parsley Salad, page 208

The Best Damn Nachos,
page 229

Stock Up the AP Way

These are the ingredients I keep on hand
to get dinner on the table quick.

PANTRY

- Beans and legumes (canned black, cannellini, and pinto beans; chickpeas; and dried red and brown lentils)

- Boxed broths (for quick soups)

- Unsweetened coconut milk

- Canned or jarred fish in oil (anchovies and tuna)

- Dried fruit (apricots, dates, and raisins)

- Grains (regular couscous, Israeli couscous, quinoa, and rice)

- Honey

- Oils (extra-virgin olive oil—both an inexpensive kind for cooking and a good one for salad dressings and for finishing dishes—canola, and coconut)

- Pasta and noodles (various shapes of regular, whole wheat, and gluten-free pasta—Banza chickpea pasta is delicious—and rice noodles)

- Polenta

- Salt (kosher and a flaky sort, like Maldon)

- Spices (particularly cayenne pepper, chili powder, ground cumin, ground coriander, mustard seeds, whole black peppercorns, smoked paprika, red pepper flakes, and ground turmeric)

- Canned tomatoes (whole and crushed) and tomato paste

- Vinegars (apple cider, red and white wine, and balsamic)

FREEZER

- Bacon

- Ground beef, lamb, and/or pork

- Nuts and seeds (almonds, cashews, hazelnuts, pine nuts, sunflower seeds, and sesame seeds; freeze for longer storage)

- Peas

- Sausages

- Shrimp

COUNTERTOP

- Garlic

- Onions

FRIDGE

- Unsalted butter
- Capers
- Cured and smoked meats (such as kielbasa, mortadella, and salami)
- Eggs
- Hot sauces (Cholula, green Tabasco, harissa, Sriracha, chili garlic, and sweet chili)
- Lemons
- Limes
- Maple syrup
- Mayo
- Miso paste
- Dijon mustard
- Nut butters
- Olives
- Hunk of Parm
- Pickles (such as bread-and-butter, cornichons, giardiniera, and pickled jalapeños)
- Sour cream
- Soy sauce
- Tahini
- Yogurt

chapter one

SALAD,
But make it Dinner

Eating vibrant, hearty _SALADS_ makes me feel like I'm making _GOOD_ life decisions.

Sicilian Tuna Salad with
Oranges & Beets
26

Smoked Trout Niçoise with
Lemony Scallion Dressing
28

Spinach Salad with Crispy Chicken,
Mushrooms & Fried Eggs
30

Warm Kale & Chicken Salad with
Toasted Hazelnuts & Croutons
33

Pork Chop, Radicchio & Apple Salad
with Dijon Vinaigrette
34

Sweet Pea Falafel Salad with
Yogurt-Tahini Dressing
36

Chicken & Celery Salad with Creamy
Herbed Dressing
38

SICILIAN TUNA
SALAD WITH
ORANGES &
BEETS, PAGE 26

SICILIAN tuna SALAD

with Oranges + Beets

A little protein quickly turns just about any favorite salad into a meal. Packaged precooked beets can be found in the produce section at most large supermarkets, or you can prep beets using your favorite cooking method. (If you don't have a preferred way, and you're Eastern European like me, just ask your grandma.) Or you can simply leave the beets out of the salad.

Cerignola and Castelvetrano olives are mild, meaty varieties. Look for them jarred or at supermarket olive bars, or use any good-quality variety you like. **SERVES 4**

½ cup shelled unsalted pistachios

6 oranges of different varieties (e.g., blood, Cara Cara, and navel), preferably chilled

2 tablespoons red wine vinegar

Kosher salt and freshly ground black pepper

¼ cup extra-virgin olive oil, plus more for drizzling

3 small cooked beets (about 9 ounces total), cut into thick rounds

1 medium fennel bulb, preferably with fronds, stalks removed and fronds reserved, halved, cored, and very thinly sliced

½ small red onion, very thinly sliced

14 to 15 ounces jarred or canned oil-packed tuna, drained

1 cup green olives, preferably Cerignola or Castelvetrano, pitted and coarsely chopped

⅓ cup loosely packed fresh mint leaves (optional, but I love)

Flaky sea salt, such as Maldon (optional)

Toast the pistachios in a medium skillet over medium-low heat, shaking the pan occasionally, until they are fragrant and lightly toasted, 5 to 7 minutes. Transfer to a cutting board and let cool, then coarsely chop.

Halve one orange and squeeze enough juice to yield ¼ cup; set aside. Using a sharp paring knife, cut the peel and pith from the remaining oranges, then slice the fruit into thick rounds.

Whisk together the orange juice, vinegar, ¼ teaspoon salt, and a generous grinding of pepper in a bowl. Whisk in the oil.

Arrange the oranges, beets, fennel, and onion on plates. Season with salt and pepper, then top with the tuna and olives.

Whisk the dressing again to blend and spoon it over the salads. Top with the pistachios, mint, if using, and fennel fronds, if you have them. Season with flaky sea salt and more pepper, if desired, and serve.

See photo previous page

SMOKED Trout NIÇOISE

with Lemony Scallion Dressing

Traditional Niçoise salad is made with tuna (which can be used here, too), but I often swap in smoked fish, a simple twist that adds rich, complex flavor. (If opting for salmon, don't substitute cold-smoked, the most common type; look for hot-smoked, which has a drier, flakier texture.) I learned the trick of tossing the potatoes with harissa from the cooks at Café Olé in Philadelphia, a lunchtime favorite during the filming of *Queer Eye*.

Harissa, a versatile North African condiment with a slightly smoky tang, is made from a combination of mild and spicy red peppers and lemon or vinegar. It's sold both as a thick paste (often in tubes) and a jarred sauce. Spice levels vary from brand to brand. Here I use the jarred version, but if you have the paste, thin it with a little warm water, and it'll work just as well. **SERVES 4**

¾ pound small or larger potatoes, cut into 1-inch chunks

Kosher salt

4 large eggs

¾ pound medium asparagus, trimmed

¼ pound green beans, trimmed

2 scallions, thinly sliced

1½ teaspoons grated lemon zest

3 tablespoons fresh lemon juice

Pinch of cayenne pepper, or to taste

¼ cup plus 2 table-spoons extra-virgin olive oil

2 tablespoons harissa (see headnote), plus more if desired

6 packed cups frisée, washed, dried, and torn into pieces, or mixed greens (about 8 ounces)

Freshly ground black pepper

8 radishes, quartered

8 ounces (about 1½ cups) Sungold, cherry, or other small tomatoes, halved

8 ounces smoked trout or mackerel or hot-smoked salmon (see headnote)

¾ cup Niçoise, Gaeta, or Greek olives, pitted

2 tablespoons capers, drained

Place the potatoes in a medium saucepan, add water to cover by 1 inch and 2 tablespoons salt, and bring to a boil. Reduce the heat and boil gently until the potatoes are fork-tender, 15 to 20 minutes for whole potatoes or 10 to 15 minutes for chunks. Drain, transfer to a plate, and set aside.

Meanwhile, bring a large saucepan of well-salted water to a boil. Gently lower in the eggs and cook at a gentle boil for 7½ minutes. Using a slotted spoon, transfer the eggs to a bowl of ice water (keep the water at a boil). Let stand for 5 minutes, then drain. Peel under running water.

Add the asparagus to the boiling water and cook until crisp-tender, 4 to 5 minutes. Use tongs to transfer the asparagus to a bowl of ice water (keep the water at a boil) and let stand for 5 minutes, then remove and pat dry. Add the green beans to the boiling water and cook until crisp-tender, 4 to 5 minutes, then drain, cool in ice water, drain again, and pat dry.

Whisk together half of the scallions, the lemon zest and juice, ¼ teaspoon salt, and the cayenne in a bowl. Add the oil and whisk well to combine. Adjust the salt and cayenne to taste.

Halve the potatoes and toss with the harissa and ¼ teaspoon salt; adjust the harissa to taste. Cut the eggs in half.

Arrange the greens on a platter or in individual shallow bowls. Sprinkle with the remaining scallions and season with a pinch each of salt and pepper. Top with the potatoes, eggs, asparagus, green beans, radishes, tomatoes, trout, olives, and capers. Drizzle with the scallion dressing, grind over some pepper, and serve.

SPINACH SALAD
with Crispy Chicken, Mushrooms + Fried Eggs

Spinach salad with eggs and bacon is a classic that I love. Keep your egg yolks runny; that way, they'll blend with the dressing for a delectable creaminess.

I like chicken thighs for this recipe, but if time is tight, you can use leftovers from the grill or a rotisserie bird. **SERVES 4**

3 tablespoons finely chopped red onion

3 tablespoons red or white wine vinegar

Kosher salt

1 teaspoon Dijon mustard

1 teaspoon honey

¼ cup extra-virgin olive oil

4 ounces thick-cut bacon (about 3 slices), cut crosswise into 1-inch-wide pieces

4 bone-in skin-on chicken thighs (about 2 pounds; see headnote)

Freshly ground black pepper

4 tablespoons (½ stick) unsalted butter

1 pound cremini or mixed wild mushrooms, stemmed if using shiitakes, caps halved or quartered if large

4 large eggs

2 large bunches spinach (about 1 pound total), washed, dried, stemmed, and torn into 2-inch pieces

2 medium Fresno or jalapeño chiles, seeded and thinly sliced

Heat the oven to 425°F, with a rack in the middle.

Combine the onion, vinegar, and ½ teaspoon salt in a medium bowl and let stand for 10 minutes. Whisk in the mustard and honey, then whisk in the oil to combine.

Cook the bacon in a large skillet over medium-high heat until crisp, 6 to 8 minutes. Using a slotted spoon, transfer the bacon to a plate, leaving the fat in the pan.

Pat the chicken dry with paper towels, then season all over with salt and pepper. Heat the fat in the skillet over medium-high heat until hot but not smoking. Add the chicken, skin side down, and cook until golden and crisp, about 8 minutes. Transfer to a baking pan, skin side up, then roast until the chicken is cooked through, 8 to 10 minutes.

Meanwhile, add 2 tablespoons of the butter to the skillet and melt it over medium-high heat. Add half of the mushrooms, season with ¼ teaspoon salt and a generous grinding of pepper, and cook, stirring occasionally, until tender, 3 to 5 minutes. Using a slotted spoon, transfer the mushrooms to a bowl that can accommodate the salad. Add 1 more tablespoon butter, the remaining mushrooms, ¼ teaspoon salt, and another grinding of pepper to the pan and cook the mushrooms in the same way. Transfer to the bowl.

Remove the chicken from the oven. Transfer to a cutting board.

Meanwhile, melt the remaining tablespoon of butter in a large nonstick skillet over medium heat. Crack in the eggs one at a time and cook until the whites are set but the yolks are still runny, about 5 minutes. Remove from the heat.

Slice the chicken from the bones (discard the bones). Cut the meat into thin strips and add to the bowl with the mushrooms. Add the spinach, dressing, and a generous pinch each of salt and pepper. Toss to combine. Adjust the seasonings to taste.

Arrange the salad on plates. Top with the eggs and chiles and serve.

Warm Kale + CHICKEN SALAD with Toasted Hazelnuts + Croutons

This filling salad looks like more work than it actually is. A warm dressing softens the kale leaves, and homemade torn croutons fancy things up a bit.

Tuscan kale (aka dinosaur kale, cavolo nero, or black kale) is slightly less bitter, with a more tender and nutty leaf, than other varieties, but any hearty salad greens can be used. Similarly, any nuts you like (or none at all) are just fine. **SERVES 4**

½ cup hazelnuts, with or without skins

About ½ cup extra-virgin olive oil

4 cups torn (1½-inch pieces) country bread

Kosher salt and freshly ground black pepper

1 small garlic clove, gently smashed and peeled

4 anchovy fillets

¼ teaspoon red pepper flakes

3 tablespoons fresh lemon juice

8 cups torn Tuscan or other kale (from a ½-pound bunch)

3 cups shredded rotisserie chicken

¼ cup raisins

Heat the oven to 350°F.

Spread the nuts on a small baking sheet and bake until fragrant and toasted, 10 to 12 minutes. If using nuts with skins, rub them in a clean towel to remove most of the skins (it's OK if they don't all come off). Let cool, then coarsely chop.

Meanwhile, heat ⅓ inch of oil in a medium skillet over medium-high heat until it ripples. Add the bread in a single layer and fry undisturbed until the pieces are lightly golden on the bottom, about 1 minute. Turn and continue frying until just lightly golden, 1 to 2 minutes more. Remove the pan from the heat and transfer the croutons to paper towels to drain. Season with salt and pepper while warm.

Remove any bread bits from the skillet, then pour the oil into a measuring cup. Add more oil as needed to make ⅓ cup, then return the oil to the skillet. Add the garlic, anchovies, and red pepper flakes and heat over medium heat until warm and fragrant, about 1 minute. Remove the pan from the heat and whisk in the lemon juice and ¼ teaspoon salt.

Combine the kale, chicken, and half of the hazelnuts and raisins in a bowl. Pour on the dressing and season with salt. Toss to combine. Arrange the salad on plates. Top with the remaining nuts and raisins and serve.

Pork Chop, RADICCHIO + APPLE Salad with Dijon Vinaigrette

Pork and apples are in a long-term, committed relationship. For this salad, pair these two lovebirds with your favorite greens. I go for a mix of kale, endive, and radicchio, but really anything works. Thin boneless pork chops (rather than thicker boneless or bone-in ones) mean less time at the stove, but you can use any chops you like and adjust the cooking time accordingly. **SERVES 4**

1½ pounds thin boneless pork chops (about ½ inch thick)

Kosher salt and freshly ground black pepper

¼ cup plus 2 tablespoons extra-virgin olive oil

2 tablespoons apple cider vinegar

2 tablespoons finely chopped red onion

1 tablespoon Dijon mustard

1 teaspoon honey

6 cups torn kale (from a ½-pound bunch)

1 medium head radicchio, leaves separated and torn (about 4 cups)

2 endives, sliced crosswise on a diagonal

1 sweet-tart apple, such as Gala or Fuji, halved, cored, and thinly sliced

3 tablespoons salted sunflower seeds, or ¼ cup chopped toasted nuts (optional)

Season the pork chops all over with salt and pepper. Heat 2 tablespoons of the oil in a large skillet over medium-high heat until hot but not smoking. Add the pork and cook, turning once, until browned and cooked through, 2 to 3 minutes per side for medium. Transfer to a cutting board and let rest for 5 to 10 minutes.

Meanwhile, combine the vinegar, onion, and ¼ teaspoon salt in a small bowl and let stand for 10 minutes. Whisk in the mustard and honey, then whisk in the remaining ¼ cup oil to combine.

Toss together the kale, radicchio, endive, apple, half of the sunflower seeds or nuts, if using, the dressing, and a generous pinch each of salt and pepper in a large bowl. Adjust the seasonings to taste.

Arrange the salad on plates. Slice the pork chops and divide among the salads. Top with the remaining sunflower seeds or nuts, if using, and serve.

SWEET PEA FALAFEL Salad

with Yogurt-Tahini Dressing

I throw peas into literally anything, my falafel included. Scattered over a salad, the golden, crispy chickpea nuggets recall croutons but are healthier, and the peas make them fresh and light. I like the light nuttiness of chickpea flour (aka garbanzo bean flour or besan), which is also great for gluten-free eaters, but all-purpose flour works just as well. Look for the former at health food stores, large supermarkets, and online.

This dressing can be used on any salad, and it also makes a great dip for crudités.

SERVES 4 TO 6

TAHINI DRESSING
- ¾ cup plain whole-milk yogurt
- ¾ teaspoon grated lemon zest
- 1 tablespoon plus 1 teaspoon fresh lemon juice
- 1 tablespoon plus 1 teaspoon well-stirred tahini
- ½ garlic clove, finely chopped
- ¼ teaspoon kosher salt
- Generous pinch of cayenne pepper

FALAFEL
- 2 (15-ounce) cans chickpeas, rinsed, drained, and patted dry
- 1½ cups thawed frozen peas
- ¾ cup finely chopped fresh cilantro, plus ¼ cup loosely packed cilantro leaves
- 1 garlic clove, gently smashed and peeled
- Kosher salt
- 1 teaspoon baking powder
- ¾ teaspoon ground cumin
- ⅛ teaspoon cayenne pepper
- ½ cup finely chopped onion
- ½ cup chickpea flour or all-purpose flour (see headnote)
- Canola oil for shallow-frying

SALAD
- 12 cups chopped romaine (1 large head)
- ½ English cucumber or 2 Persian cucumbers, cubed
- 1 cup cherry tomatoes, halved
- ½ cup loosely packed fresh mint leaves (optional, but I love!)
- Kosher salt and freshly ground black pepper
- Micro sprouts for topping (optional)

For the dressing: Whisk together all of the ingredients with 3 tablespoons cold water in a bowl to combine. Adjust the seasonings to taste. Refrigerate until ready to use.

For the falafel: Heat the oven to 200°F. Line a large plate with paper towels.

Pulse the chickpeas, peas, chopped cilantro, garlic, 1 teaspoon salt, the baking powder, cumin, and cayenne in a food processor 5 or 6 times. Scrape down the sides of the bowl. Repeat once or twice, until the mixture is well combined but not pureed to a paste. Transfer to a bowl and stir in the onion and chickpea flour to combine.

Form scant ¼-cupfuls of the falafel batter into patties about 2½ inches in diameter and ½ inch thick, arranging them on a large plate or baking sheet as you go; you should have 16 patties.

Heat ½ inch of oil in a large skillet over medium-high heat until hot but not smoking—350° to 375°F on a deep-fry thermometer, if you have one (tilt the pan to pool the oil to test it). If you don't have a thermometer, test the oil with a teaspoon of batter; when the oil is ready, the batter will sizzle and bubble on contact. Fry the falafel in 2 batches, turning once, until golden on both sides and cooked through, about 3 minutes per side, then transfer to the paper towels to drain and season with salt. Transfer the first batch to a baking sheet and keep warm in the oven while you cook the remaining falafel.

For the salad: Arrange the salad ingredients on plates, including the mint, if using. Season generously with salt and pepper.

Top the salads with the warm falafel. Drizzle with the dressing, top with micro sprouts, if using, and serve.

Chicken + Celery SALAD
with Creamy Herbed Dressing

This lightened version of a classic chicken salad calls up a daydream: I see myself eating it on a warm summer night on the wraparound porch of the Connecticut home I don't have, as my trio of golden retrievers (which I also don't have) chase each other on the front lawn. Seriously though, the dish is great for an outdoor party or picnic. If you're taking it on the road, pack the dressing in a jar and toss it into your bag with a cold pack.

Any cooked chicken—poached, grilled, or rotisserie—works well here. If you prefer, use mint or basil instead of the tarragon. **SERVES 4**

DRESSING

½ cup sour cream

2 tablespoons chopped fresh tarragon, basil, or mint

½ teaspoon grated lemon zest

1½ tablespoons fresh lemon juice

1 tablespoon mayonnaise

Kosher salt and freshly ground black pepper

SALAD

½ cup walnut halves

1 pound boneless, skinless chicken breasts, cooked and sliced (about 3 cups)

1 head Bibb, Boston, or butter lettuce, leaves separated

1 bunch spinach (about 8 ounces), tough stems removed, leaves torn if large

2 celery stalks, thinly sliced, plus 1⅓ cups loosely packed celery leaves

Heat the oven to 350°F.

For the dressing: Stir together the sour cream, tarragon, lemon zest and juice, mayonnaise, ¼ teaspoon salt, a generous grinding of pepper, and 2 teaspoons water in a bowl.

For the salad: Spread the walnuts on a small baking sheet and bake until fragrant and toasted, 10 to 12 minutes. Transfer to a plate and let cool, then coarsely chop.

Arrange the chicken, lettuce, spinach, and celery on plates. Season with salt. Drizzle with the dressing, top with the nuts, and serve.

chapter two
VEGGIE
Nights

Satisfyingly decadent, exciting + VEGGIE-PACKED, these dishes cover all the bases, whether I want to go VEGAN or just follow a meatless script.

White Bean & Cauliflower Soup with Herby Oil
44

Red Lentil Soup with Ginger & Coconut
49

Miso Noodle Soup with Mushrooms, Peas & Greens
50

Chickpea, Quinoa & White Bean Chili
54

Mushroom Mapo Tofu with Water Chestnuts
57

Coconut-Cauliflower Korma
60

Golden Root Vegetable Potpie
62

Roasted Cabbage Steaks
with Apple-Dijon Vinaigrette
65

Chili-Roasted Winter Squash
with Lentils, Lime & Arugula
66

Lazy Pierogies with Wild Mushrooms,
Cabbage & Prunes
69

Crispy Curry Tofu with Arugula Salad

WHITE BEAN + Cauliflower Soup with Herby Oil

For this soup, I roast the cauliflower to bring out its sweetness. Then it's a quick finish in the pot with canned beans and wilted greens. A drizzle of herby olive oil just before serving makes it special. If you're not going full vegan, shave some Parmigiano over the top for a tasty final touch. **SERVES 4 TO 6**

1 large head cauliflower, cut into ½-inch pieces (including leaves and stem)

1 medium red onion, coarsely chopped

1 garlic clove, gently smashed, peeled, and halved

¼ teaspoon red pepper flakes

½ cup plus 2 tablespoons extra-virgin olive oil

Kosher salt and freshly ground black pepper

¼ cup finely chopped soft fresh herbs (one or more of the following: basil, chives, cilantro, tarragon, or scallions)

½ teaspoon grated lemon zest

1 quart low-sodium vegetable broth

2 (15-ounce) cans cannellini or other white beans, rinsed and drained

1 pound hearty greens, such as kale, chard, or escarole, or a mix, chopped

Lemon wedges for serving

Shaved or grated Parmigiano-Reggiano cheese for serving (optional)

Heat the oven to 450°F, with the racks in the upper and lower thirds. Line two baking sheets with parchment paper.

Divide the cauliflower, onion, and garlic between the baking sheets and sprinkle with the red pepper flakes. Toss each pan of vegetables with 2 tablespoons of the oil, ¼ teaspoon salt, and a grinding of pepper. Roast, rotating the baking sheets halfway through, until the cauliflower is lightly golden and tender but still has a slight bite, 30 to 35 minutes.

Meanwhile, stir together the remaining ¼ cup plus 2 tablespoons oil, the herbs, lemon zest, and a generous pinch of salt in a bowl.

Transfer the roasted vegetables, including any oil and little bits, to a large wide pot. Add the broth, beans, and 3 cups water and bring to a simmer. Add the greens and cook until wilted, 1 to 2 minutes. Remove from the heat and adjust the seasonings to taste.

Ladle the soup into bowls. Give each a squeeze of lemon juice, then drizzle the soup with the herb oil, top with cheese, if using, season with pepper, and serve.

Red Lentil SOUP
with Ginger + Coconut

This soup just happens to be vegan—I didn't plan it that way. Fresh ginger and a host of pantry spices give it a warm vibe. Sweet potato makes it a meal. **SERVES 4 TO 6**

- 2 tablespoons unrefined coconut oil or extra-virgin olive oil
- 1 medium onion, chopped
- 2 garlic cloves, thinly sliced
- 3 tablespoons finely chopped peeled fresh ginger
- 1¼ teaspoons ground turmeric
- 1 teaspoon ground cumin
- ¾ teaspoon ground coriander
- ¼ teaspoon ground cinnamon
- ⅛ teaspoon cayenne pepper, plus more for serving (optional)
- Kosher salt and freshly ground black pepper
- 1 large sweet potato, peeled and cut into ½-inch cubes (about 3 cups)
- 1 (13.5-ounce) can coconut milk, well shaken
- 1 cup dried red lentils
- 1 (14.5-ounce) can crushed tomatoes
- Chopped fresh cilantro (optional) and lime wedges for serving

Heat the oil in a medium saucepan over medium heat. Add the onion, garlic, and ginger and cook, stirring occasionally, until the onion begins to soften, about 5 minutes. Stir in the turmeric, cumin, coriander, cinnamon, cayenne, 1 teaspoon salt, and several grinds of pepper. Cook, stirring, until fragrant, about 2 minutes. Stir in the sweet potato and cook for 1 minute more.

Set aside ¼ cup of the coconut milk for serving. Add the remaining coconut milk to the saucepan and stir with a wooden spoon, scraping up any browned bits from the bottom of the pan. Stir in the lentils, tomatoes, 4 cups water, and ¼ teaspoon salt and bring to a boil, then reduce the heat to low and simmer, stirring occasionally, until the lentils are tender, 20 to 25 minutes.

Ladle the soup into bowls. Drizzle with the reserved coconut milk. Top with cilantro and a grinding of black pepper or more cayenne, if desired. Serve with lime wedges.

MISO NOODLE SOUP

with Mushrooms, Peas + Greens

I often preach the gospel of saving a splash or two of the starchy water from cooking pasta because of the magical way it lends body to the sauce. In Japan, drinking the soba-noodle water, called *soba-yu,* is part of the pleasure of the meal. The earthy, nutty liquid is said to offer the same beneficial nutrients (antioxidants, essential amino acids, and more) found in the noodles themselves.

For this soup, I use the soba cooking water and some miso paste as the base. Be gentle with your miso, and add it off the heat: High temps kill its beneficial live bacteria and probiotics. If you're not serving all the soup at once, either add the miso proportionally or very gently reheat the soup later on. **SERVES 4**

5 ounces soba noodles

3 tablespoons toasted sesame oil, plus more for drizzling

3 garlic cloves, gently smashed and peeled

2 tablespoons finely chopped peeled fresh ginger

1 pound mixed wild mushrooms, stemmed if using shiitakes, caps halved or quartered if large

Kosher salt

2 cups frozen peas, thawed

5 ounces baby spinach, mizuna, tatsoi, or mixed Asian greens

¼ cup white miso paste

1 tablespoon soy sauce, plus more for serving

4 scallions, thinly sliced

Red pepper flakes, toasted sesame seeds, and/or micro greens for topping (optional)

Cook the noodles in boiling water according to the package instructions. Drain in a colander placed over a large bowl. Set aside the soba water. Rinse the noodles under cold water, drain, and set aside.

Measure the soba water and add more water if needed to make 8 cups. (Or discard any extra soba water.)

Heat the oil in a large wide saucepan over medium-high heat. Add the garlic and ginger and cook, stirring frequently, until fragrant, about 1 minute. Stir in the mushrooms with a generous pinch of salt. Cook, stirring occasionally, until tender, about 5 minutes. Stir in the peas and cook for 1 minute. Add the soba water, increase the heat to high, and bring just to a low boil. Stir in the greens and immediately remove from the heat.

Scoop ¼ cup of the broth into a bowl and whisk in the miso. Return the mixture to the soup, add the soy sauce, and stir to combine.

Divide the noodles among four bowls. Ladle the soup over them. Top with the scallions. Drizzle over sesame oil and soy sauce, and top with red pepper flakes, sesame seeds, and micro greens, if desired.

CHICKPEA,
QUINOA &
WHITE BEAN
CHILI, PAGE 54

CHICKPEA, Quinoa + WHITE BEAN Chili

This vegan chili has lots of the same flavors that make the meaty kind so satisfying. Quinoa, rich in protein, adds texture. If you can get them, fire-roasted tomatoes lend great charred notes. Pile on your favorite toppings. **SERVES 4 TO 6**

3 tablespoons olive oil

1 large onion, coarsely chopped

1 large red bell pepper, cored, seeded, and chopped

3 garlic cloves, finely chopped

Kosher salt

2 tablespoons tomato paste

1 tablespoon chili powder

2 teaspoons ground cumin

1½ teaspoons dried oregano

1 (28-ounce) can crushed tomatoes, preferably fire-roasted

1 (15-ounce) can cannellini or other beans, rinsed and drained

1 (15-ounce can) chickpeas, rinsed and drained

1 tablespoon finely chopped chipotle chiles in adobo, plus more to taste

2 teaspoons packed brown sugar (light or dark)

½ cup quinoa (tricolor or any color), rinsed

OPTIONAL TOPPINGS
Coarsely crushed tortilla chips, sour cream, shredded cheddar or pepper Jack cheese, sliced or cubed avocado, sliced scallions, sliced fresh or pickled jalapeños, and/or chopped fresh cilantro

Heat the oil in a Dutch oven or other large heavy-bottomed pot over medium heat. Add the onion, bell pepper, garlic, and 1 teaspoon salt and cook, stirring frequently, until the vegetables are softened, about 8 minutes.

Meanwhile, dissolve the tomato paste in 2½ cups water. Stir the chili powder, cumin, and oregano into the onion mixture and cook, stirring, until the spices begin to stick to the bottom of the pot, about 1 minute. Add the tomatoes, beans, chickpeas, chipotles, brown sugar, 1 teaspoon salt, and the tomato paste mixture. Increase the heat to medium-high and cook, stirring occasionally, until the mixture reaches a low boil. Add the quinoa, reduce the heat to maintain a simmer, and cook, stirring occasionally, until the quinoa is tender, about 25 minutes.

Remove the chili from the heat and adjust the seasonings and chipotle to taste. Add water to thin, if desired. Serve with your favorite toppings.

See photo previous page

MUSHROOM mapo tofu with Water Chestnuts

Chopped mushrooms are meaty stand-ins for ground beef in this vegan version of a popular Sichuan tofu stir-fry. The rich sauce gets its mouth-tingling spice from Sichuan peppercorns.

If you're using shiitakes and the stems are very fresh and tender, you can include them as well as the caps in the dish; otherwise, remove them and save them to make broth. Broad bean paste, aka *doubanjiang*, is a salty paste made from fermented beans, soybeans, rice, and spices. Look for it at Asian markets or online. The SOEOS brand makes a vegan version. Black bean garlic sauce, found in the Asian section of many supermarkets, can be used in a pinch; the dish will be a little different, but still good. **SERVES 4**

1½ cups jasmine or other long-grain white rice

1 pound shiitake or baby bella mushrooms, or a mix, trimmed (see headnote) and halved, or quartered if large

1 bunch scallions, thinly sliced

3 tablespoons canola oil

4 garlic cloves, finely chopped

3 tablespoons finely chopped peeled fresh ginger (from a 2-inch knob)

1 teaspoon whole Sichuan peppercorns or ½ teaspoon freshly ground black pepper

¼ cup Sichuan broad bean paste (see headnote) or black bean garlic sauce

1 pound silken tofu, drained and cut into 1-inch pieces

1 (8-ounce) can water chestnuts, drained

Fresh basil leaves, torn if large (optional, but I love), and toasted sesame oil for serving

Cook the rice according to the package instructions.

Meanwhile, pulse the mushrooms in a food processor until finely chopped.

Set ¼ cup of the scallions aside for serving. Heat the oil in a Dutch oven or other large heavy-bottomed pot over medium-high heat until hot. Add the mushrooms and cook, stirring frequently, until tender, about 5 minutes. Add the remaining scallions, the garlic, ginger, and Sichuan peppercorns and cook, stirring, until fragrant, about 1 minute.

Add the bean paste and 1½ cups water to the pot and stir to combine. Bring to a simmer, add the tofu and water chestnuts, and cook, stirring occasionally, until warmed through, about 2 minutes.

Serve the mapo tofu over the rice, topped with the reserved scallions, basil, if using, and a drizzling of sesame oil.

COCONUT-CAULIFLOWER
KORMA, PAGE 60

Coconut-
CAULIFLOWER
Korma

This mild, quick, one-pot Indian-inspired curry gets its creaminess from coconut milk, a pantry stalwart that plays well with ginger and curry flavors. Extra coconut love comes in the form of a crunchy toasted coconut flake topping. (If toasted coconut chips are available at your market, you can skip the toasting step.) If you like dairy, enjoy the korma with yogurt or buttered naan.

SERVES 4 TO 6

½ cup unsweetened flaked dried coconut (aka coconut chips; optional)

2 tablespoons extra-virgin olive oil

1 large onion, chopped

4 garlic cloves, finely chopped

2 tablespoons chopped peeled fresh ginger

Kosher salt

1 large head cauliflower (about 1¾ pounds), trimmed, florets cut into bite-sized pieces, stem coarsely chopped

2 tablespoons mild curry powder

1 teaspoon ground turmeric

¼ teaspoon cayenne pepper, plus more for serving

2 (13.5-ounce) cans full-fat coconut milk, well shaken

1 (15-ounce) can chickpeas, rinsed and drained

1 medium serrano or small jalapeño chile, halved lengthwise (optional)

¾ cup raisins, preferably golden

Lime wedges for serving

FOR SERVING (OPTIONAL)

Steamed rice or warm buttered pita, naan, or other flatbread

Plain yogurt, fruit chutney, and/ or chopped fresh cilantro

If using coconut flakes, heat the oven to 300°F, with a rack in the middle.

Spread the coconut on a small baking sheet and bake until lightly golden, 5 to 7 minutes. Remove from the oven and let cool.

Heat the oil in a Dutch oven or other large heavy-bottomed pot over medium-high heat until hot. Add the onion, garlic, ginger, and ½ teaspoon salt and cook, stirring often, until the onion is softened, about 5 minutes. Add the cauliflower with ½ teaspoon salt and cook, stirring occasionally, until it begins to soften, about 5 minutes. Add the curry powder, turmeric, and cayenne and cook, stirring occasionally, until fragrant, about 3 minutes.

Stir in the coconut milk, chickpeas, chile, if using, raisins, and ¾ teaspoon salt. Bring to a simmer and cook, stirring occasionally, until the cauliflower is tender and the liquid is slightly reduced, 20 to 25 minutes. Remove from the heat and adjust the seasonings to taste.

Serve warm, over rice or with flatbread alongside, if you like. Top the korma with a squeeze of lime and a sprinkling of cayenne, along with yogurt, chutney, cilantro, and/or toasted coconut, if desired.

See photo previous page

GOLDEN ROOT VEGETABLE Potpie

For a Meatless Monday when you want to stick to the script, or for any day you prefer vegetables to meat, this creamy potpie is the perfect meal. The flexible mix of vegetables means you can try something new from the farmers' market or use up any veg-drawer stragglers. Baking the puff pastry separately keeps it from getting soggy.

For an added creative twist, sprinkle the top of the pastry with everything bagel seasoning mix, which can be found in the spice section at Trader Joe's and other grocery stores. **SERVES 4**

PUFF PASTRY

1 sheet frozen puff pastry (half a 17-ounce package), thawed

1 large egg, beaten with 1 teaspoon water for egg wash

Kosher salt and freshly ground black pepper

VEG FILLING

4 tablespoons (½ stick) unsalted butter

6 cups cubed (⅓-inch) mixed root vegetables, such as carrots, parsnips, rutabaga, peeled butternut or kabocha squash, sweet potato, and/or celery root

1 cup frozen pearl onions, thawed

2 garlic cloves, thinly sliced

2 teaspoons finely chopped fresh rosemary or ¾ teaspoon dried

1½ teaspoons kosher salt

1¼ teaspoons ground turmeric

¼ teaspoon cayenne pepper (or black pepper)

1 (13.5-ounce) can full-fat coconut milk, well shaken

2 tablespoons all-purpose flour

1 cup (8 ounces) sour cream

2 tablespoons fresh lime or lemon juice

Heat the oven to 400°F, with a rack in the lower third. Line a baking sheet with parchment paper.

Unfold the pastry onto a lightly floured work surface. Cut into eight 2¼- by- 4½-inch rectangles and place on the prepared baking sheet. Brush the tops with the egg wash and sprinkle with salt and pepper. Bake until puffed and golden, 12 to 15 minutes. Remove from the oven and let cool.

While the pastry is baking, melt 2½ tablespoons of the butter in a large wide saucepan over medium-high heat. Add the firmer root vegetables (carrots, parsnips, rutabaga), onions, garlic, rosemary, and salt and cook, stirring occasionally, until the onions are softened, 6 to 8 minutes.

Stir in the turmeric and cayenne, then add the remaining root vegetables, the coconut milk, and 1 cup water. Partially cover and cook until the vegetables are just tender, about 8 minutes.

Meanwhile, melt the remaining 1½ tablespoons butter in a small skillet or saucepan over medium heat. Stir in the flour, reduce the heat to low, and cook, stirring constantly, for 3 minutes to remove the floury taste. Remove from the heat.

When the vegetables are just tender, scrape the flour mixture into the pot (get every bit) and stir well, then stir in the sour cream. Bring the mixture to a gentle simmer and cook, stirring occasionally, until the vegetables are tender and the sauce is thick enough to coat the back of a spoon, 8 to 10 minutes. Stir in the lime or lemon juice and adjust the seasonings to taste. Remove from the heat.

To assemble: Place one piece of puff pastry, golden side down, in each of four shallow bowls. Top with the filling and the remaining pieces of puff pastry, golden side up. Serve immediately.

Roasted CABBAGE STEAKS
with Apple-Dijon Vinaigrette

Cabbage is having a moment, which means that by default Poland is too, because the cold-climate crucifer is basically our national food. Cutting it into slabs and roasting it gives it crisp, caramelized edges and a tender bite.

Using applesauce in the vinaigrette is a new trick for a classic pantry staple; its tart, fruity notes bring a sweet brightness to the dish. **SERVES 4**

CABBAGE STEAKS

1 medium red cabbage, trimmed

¼ cup extra-virgin olive oil

½ teaspoon dried herbes de Provence, thyme, or oregano

Kosher salt and freshly ground black pepper

½ cup walnut pieces

1 cup quinoa, rinsed and drained

1 bay leaf

VINAIGRETTE

3 tablespoons applesauce

1 tablespoon apple cider vinegar

1 teaspoon Dijon mustard

1 teaspoon honey

¼ teaspoon kosher salt

⅛ teaspoon freshly ground black pepper

⅓ cup extra-virgin olive oil

3 tablespoons raisins, chopped dried apricots, dried cherries, or chopped dates

1 cup coarsely chopped fresh flat-leaf parsley

Flaky sea salt, such as Maldon (optional)

4 ounces soft goat cheese for serving (optional)

For the cabbage steaks: Heat the oven to 425°F. Line a baking sheet with parchment paper.

Cut about ½ inch from one long side of the cabbage to create a flat edge (so it won't roll) and place cut side down on the cutting board. Cut four ½-inch-thick lengthwise slices from the middle of the cabbage outward (to get the largest pieces) to make cabbage "steaks" (reserve the remaining cabbage for another use). Arrange the steaks on the prepared baking sheet with the core ends toward the corners of the pan so they get the most heat. Brush with the oil. Season with the dried herbs, ½ teaspoon salt, and ¼ teaspoon pepper.

Cover the pan tightly with foil and roast for 25 minutes. Uncover and continue roasting until the cabbage steaks are golden and tender, 25 to 30 minutes more.

Meanwhile, spread the nuts on a small baking sheet and bake until fragrant, 7 to 9 minutes. Transfer to a plate and let cool, then coarsely chop.

To cook the quinoa, bring 2 cups water to a boil in a medium saucepan. Add the quinoa along with the bay leaf, reduce the heat to low, cover, and simmer until tender, about 10 minutes. Drain any excess water. Remove and discard the bay leaf. Season the quinoa to taste with salt and pepper and set aside.

For the vinaigrette: Whisk together the applesauce, vinegar, Dijon, honey, salt, and pepper in a small bowl. Whisk in the oil.

When the cabbage is ready, sprinkle the dried fruit over the top, return the pan to the oven, and cook for about 5 minutes more to plump the fruit a bit.

Spoon the quinoa onto plates, spreading it out a bit. Arrange the cabbage steaks on top. Drizzle with the vinaigrette. Top with the nuts, parsley, and, if desired, flaky salt to taste, and then the cheese, if using.

Chili–Roasted WINTER SQUASH
with Lentils, Lime + Arugula

If you don't know what to do with winter squash other than make it into soup, this recipe is for you. For many varieties of squash, peeling is unnecessary. The skin becomes tender once roasted, tastes good, and looks nice on the plate. If you don't want to eat it, it's easy to remove it after roasting. **SERVES 4 TO 6**

2 to 2½ pounds winter squash (kabocha, acorn, delicata, or peeled butternut), halved, seeded, and cut into ½-inch-thick wedges (or if delicata, into rounds)

10 leafy thyme sprigs

2 teaspoons chili powder

½ cup plus 2 table-spoons extra-virgin olive oil

Kosher salt and freshly ground black pepper

2 medium red onions, trimmed, leaving some of the root end intact, and cut into ½-inch-thick wedges

¼ cup fresh lime juice (from 2 or 3 large limes)

2 tablespoons finely chopped shallot or red onion

½ cup dried brown lentils or French green lentils

8 cups (4 ounces) loosely packed baby arugula or other baby greens

OPTIONAL TOPPINGS

½ cup roasted salted pepitas

4 ounces goat cheese or feta cheese, crumbled (1 cup)

Heat the oven to 425°F. Line two baking sheets with parchment paper.

Toss together the squash, thyme sprigs, chili powder, 2 tablespoons of the oil, ¾ teaspoon salt, and ¼ teaspoon pepper in a large bowl. Spread the squash out on the baking sheets in a single layer, cut side down.

In the same bowl, toss together the onion wedges, 1 tablespoon oil, ¼ teaspoon salt, and a generous pinch of pepper. Arrange the onion wedges on the baking sheets with the squash.

Roast the vegetables, rotating the pans and switching their positions halfway through, until golden and tender, 40 to 45 minutes. Remove from the oven.

Meanwhile, combine the lime juice, chopped shallots, and ¼ teaspoon salt in a small bowl. Set aside to soften the shallots.

Combine the lentils and 1 teaspoon salt in a saucepan, add water to cover by 2 inches, and bring to a simmer. Cover and simmer until the lentils are tender but still a bit firm to the bite, 25 to 30 minutes.

Drain the lentils and spread on a baking sheet or large plate to cool.

Whisk ¼ cup plus 2 tablespoons oil into the lime juice mixture to combine.

Arrange the greens on plates. Arrange the roasted vegetables over the greens. Drizzle the remaining 1 tablespoon oil over the lentils and season with salt to taste, then spoon them onto the plates. Drizzle the dressing on top. Sprinkle with the pepitas and cheese, if desired, and more black pepper to taste.

LAZY PIEROGIES
with Wild Mushrooms, Cabbage + Prunes

These tender Polish dumplings are rather like gnocchi. They're called *leniwe* (lazy) because they're made without a filling. When I was growing up, my parents used to serve me a version of these, sprinkled with bread crumbs and sugar, to keep me from missing them when they went out on a Saturday night. Dessert for dinner—worked every time! This savory rendition of my childhood favorite pays homage to those memories, blending earthy mushrooms and tender cabbage with the brown sugar notes of chopped prunes. **SERVES 4 TO 6**

PIEROGIES

12 ounces (1¼ cups) whole milk ricotta or farmer's cheese, at room temperature

2 large eggs, at room temperature

¾ teaspoon kosher salt

1 tablespoon unsalted butter, melted and cooled

1¾ cups all-purpose flour, plus more for dusting

VEGETABLES

5 tablespoons unsalted butter

5 cups thinly sliced cabbage

¼ teaspoon kosher salt

1 pound shiitake or mixed wild mushrooms, stemmed if using shiitakes, mushroom caps halved or quartered if large

¾ cup coarsely chopped pitted prunes

3 tablespoons finely chopped fresh dill, plus more for serving

3 tablespoons coarsely chopped fresh flat-leaf parsley, plus more for serving (optional)

Freshly ground black pepper

For the pierogies: Bring a large wide pot of well-salted water to a boil. Whisk together the cheese, eggs, salt, and butter in a large bowl. Add the flour and stir to form a sticky dough.

On a floured surface, roll about a quarter of the dough into a 1-inch-thick rope, then cut the rope on a diagonal into 1-inch pieces. Repeat with the remaining dough.

Cook the dumplings in 2 batches in the boiling water until they rise to the surface, then cook for 1 minute more. Using a slotted spoon, transfer to a bowl.

For the vegetables: Melt 4 tablespoons of the butter in a large skillet over medium-high heat. Add the cabbage and salt and cook, stirring occasionally, until the cabbage is wilted, 5 to 7 minutes.

Add the mushrooms and cook, stirring occasionally, until they are tender, 6 to 8 minutes. Stir in the prunes and cook for 1 minute more.

Add the pierogies, dill, parsley, and remaining 1 tablespoon butter and toss to coat the dumplings. Heat to warm through, about 1 minute. Adjust the seasonings to taste.

Spoon the pierogies into bowls, top with more dill and parsley, if using, and serve.

CRISPY CURRY
TOFU WITH
ARUGULA SALAD,
PAGE 72

CRISPY Curry Tofu with ARUGULA SALAD

You don't need to deep-fry to get crunch. Pressing the water from tofu before panfrying it is the trick to a crispy golden exterior and a soft, custardy interior. Pile the tofu on top of greens and lemony yogurt and scatter over some sunflower seeds, and you get a riot of textures and flavors. **SERVES 4**

1 (14-ounce) package extra-firm tofu, drained

¾ cup plain Greek yogurt

1½ teaspoons grated lemon zest

1 tablespoon plus ½ teaspoon fresh lemon juice

2 tablespoons plus ¼ teaspoon curry powder

Kosher salt

⅛ teaspoon cayenne pepper

1 tablespoon extra-virgin olive oil

Canola oil for cooking

3 cups loosely packed arugula (or mâche or other tender greens)

1 medium fennel bulb, trimmed, halved, cored, and thinly sliced, or 3 cups more greens

2 scallions, thinly sliced on a long diagonal

2 tablespoons salted sunflower seeds

Cut the tofu block lengthwise in half, then crosswise into ½-inch-thick slices. Line a cutting board with a couple of paper towels and arrange the tofu squares on the paper towels. Top with a few layers of paper towels and a heavy skillet and let stand for 15 minutes to remove as much moisture as possible, then remove the wet paper towels and pat the tofu dry with fresh paper towels.

Meanwhile, stir together the yogurt, lemon zest, 1½ teaspoons of the lemon juice, ¼ teaspoon of the curry powder, ⅛ teaspoon salt, and the cayenne pepper in a bowl. Set aside.

For the dressing, whisk together the oil, the remaining 2 teaspoons lemon juice, and ¼ teaspoon salt in a bowl large enough to hold the salad. Set aside.

Combine the remaining 2 tablespoons curry powder and 1 teaspoon salt in a wide shallow bowl. Dredge the tofu in the spice mixture, gently pressing to adhere, then shake off the excess and place on a plate.

Heat 1 tablespoon canola oil in a large nonstick skillet over medium-high heat. Cook the tofu in 2 batches, turning once, until golden and crispy all over, 3 to 4 minutes per side, adding more oil between batches if needed.

Spread the yogurt in the center of four plates. Arrange the tofu on top.

Add the arugula, fennel, and scallions to the dressing and toss well. Mound the salad over the tofu. Top with the sunflower seeds and serve.

See photo previous page

chapter three
BREAK AN EGG

A good soft scramble
should be in everyone's
dinner repertoire.

Cheesy Polenta with Eggs,
Mushrooms & Thyme
79

Creamy Soft-Scrambled Eggs
with Shrimp & Scallions
82

Masala Spinach Omelette
85

Chorizo & Potato Frittata
with Asparagus & Smoky Lemon Aioli
86

Breakfast-for-Dinner Pizza
with Eggs, Zucchini & Spicy Salami
89

Egg Curry with Green Beans
90

My Favorite Shakshuka
94

Pork & Egg Rice Bowl (Katsudon)
98

CHEESY Polenta with EGGS, mushrooms + Thyme

Regular polenta tastes much more satisfying, sweeter, and nuttier than instant. Cooking it is just a thirty-minute proposition, which is the time it takes to prep the other ingredients for this dish. **SERVES 4**

1 quart low-sodium chicken broth

1½ cups polenta (not quick-cooking), coarse cornmeal, or corn grits

Kosher salt

4 tablespoons (½ stick) unsalted butter, cut into 4 pieces

¼ cup plus 3 tablespoons extra-virgin olive oil

12 ounces cremini, shiitake, or other wild mushrooms, stemmed if using shiitakes, caps halved or quartered if large

¾ teaspoon coarsely chopped fresh thyme, or ¼ teaspoon dried

Freshly ground black pepper

2 tablespoons thinly sliced fresh basil leaves, plus more for serving

¼ teaspoon red pepper flakes

5 ounces Parmigiano-Reggiano, grated (1½ cups) plus more for serving

4 large eggs

Bring the broth and 1½ cups water to a simmer in a large saucepan. Gradually stir in the polenta, add ¼ teaspoon salt, and simmer, stirring frequently, until thick, about 30 minutes.

Meanwhile, heat 1 tablespoon of the butter and 2 tablespoons of the oil in a medium skillet over medium-high heat until the butter is melted. Add the mushrooms, ½ teaspoon of the fresh thyme or ⅛ teaspoon dried, ¼ teaspoon salt, and a generous grinding of pepper. Cook, stirring occasionally, until the mushrooms are tender, 6 to 8 minutes.

While the mushrooms cook, stir together the remaining 5 tablespoons oil, the remaining ¼ teaspoon fresh thyme or ⅛ teaspoon dried, the basil, and the red pepper flakes in a small bowl. Set aside.

Stir the cheese and the remaining 3 tablespoons butter into the cooked polenta. Season with salt and pepper. Remove from the heat and cover to keep warm.

Fill a large skillet two-thirds full with water, salt it, and bring to a gentle simmer. One at a time, crack each egg into a cup and gently tip it into the simmering water. Poach the eggs until the whites are set but the yolks are still soft, 3 to 4 minutes.

Spoon the polenta into bowls. Top each one with a poached egg. Spoon the mushrooms on top, then drizzle with the herb oil. Season with salt and pepper and top with basil and more cheese.

Creamy SOFT-SCRAMBLED EGGS
with Shrimp + Scallions

A soft scramble is easier to prepare than a French omelette, its cousin, but chic enough to be dinner. I sometimes make this with crab, which is a tasty albeit fancy option, but unless you have access to the premium stuff, the dish can easily fall flat. Good-quality shrimp, on the other hand, are a great freezer basic, and their sweet, saline flavor complements the creamy eggs. Serve toasted bread and salad alongside, and you have a quick yet elegant meal. **SERVES 2 OR 3**

1 lemon

5 whole black peppercorns

1 bay leaf (optional)

Kosher salt

4 ounces large fresh or thawed frozen shrimp, peeled and deveined

6 large eggs

2 teaspoons extra-virgin olive oil

¼ cup sour cream

1 large scallion, thinly sliced

Freshly ground black pepper

Toasted sliced crusty bread for serving (optional)

Cut one slice from the lemon and set the lemon aside. Fill a medium saucepan halfway with water. Add the lemon slice, peppercorns, bay leaf, if using, and 1 teaspoon salt and bring to a boil. Add the shrimp and immediately remove the pan from the heat. Cover and let stand until the shrimp are opaque and cooked through, about 3 minutes, then drain in a sieve and run under cold water to cool them. Pat dry and finely chop.

In a large bowl, beat together the eggs, a generous pinch of salt, and 2 teaspoons water.

In a large nonstick skillet, heat the oil over medium-high heat until hot but not smoking. Add the eggs, reduce the heat to medium-low, and, using a heatproof spatula, stir vigorously and constantly until the eggs just begin to scramble, about 1 minute. Fold in the shrimp and cook until the eggs are just barely set, 30 seconds to 1 minute more.

Divide the eggs among two or three plates and dollop with the sour cream. Top with the scallion, season with pepper, and grate a little lemon zest over the top. Serve with toasted bread, if desired.

Masala SPINACH OMELETTE

Because it isn't folded or rolled like a classic omelette, this open-faced beauty requires no fussing or fancy wrist work. Mustard seeds add a lightly peppery pop, and mango chutney spooned on top brings a little sweetness. Great with a salad, this dish is also one of my favorite late-night dinners. **SERVES 2**

5 large eggs

1 scallion, chopped

¼ cup coarsely chopped fresh cilantro

Kosher salt

Pinch of cayenne pepper (optional)

¾ teaspoon whole mustard seeds (yellow or black)

½ teaspoon ground turmeric

⅛ teaspoon ground cumin

⅛ teaspoon ground ginger

½ tablespoon unsalted butter

2½ cups packed baby spinach (2½ ounces)

2 tablespoons finely chopped red onion

Warm buttered pita, naan, or other flatbread and mango chutney for serving

Beat together the eggs, scallion, cilantro, ¼ teaspoon salt, and the cayenne pepper, if using, in a medium bowl.

Mix together the mustard seeds, turmeric, cumin, and ginger in a small cup.

Melt half of the butter in a large nonstick skillet over medium-high heat. Add the spinach, onion, and spice mixture and cook, stirring frequently, until the spinach is wilted, about 3 minutes. Transfer to a plate and let cool for 5 minutes, then stir into the eggs.

Melt the remaining butter in the same skillet over medium-high heat. Ladle half of the egg mixture (about ½ cup) into the center of the pan and stir vigorously with a heatproof spatula for 5 seconds. As soon they begin to set, lift and move the pan around, swirling, so the runny egg fills in the crevices and forms a round omelette. Run a spatula around the edges of the omelette to loosen them and cook just until set yet still a little loose on top, 1 to 2 minutes.

Slide the omelette onto a plate. Repeat the process using the butter left in the pan to make the second omelette. Serve immediately, with flatbread and chutney.

CHORIZO + POTATO Frittata

with Asparagus + Smoky Lemon Aioli

This frittata was inspired by my love for the Spanish tortilla—a very thick omelette full of paper-thin slices of potatoes that have been slowly simmered in olive oil. My version, made with cubed potatoes and chorizo, is Spanish in spirit, but quicker and less fussy. It's good with a side of boiled asparagus and aioli. **SERVES 4**

AIOLI

½ small garlic clove

⅛ teaspoon kosher salt

¾ cup mayonnaise

1 teaspoon grated lemon zest

1 tablespoon fresh lemon juice

¼ teaspoon smoked paprika

FRITTATA AND ASPARAGUS

Kosher salt

2 tablespoons extra-virgin olive oil

1¼ cups cubed (¼-inch) Spanish (cured) chorizo (5 ounces)

2 cups cubed (¼-inch) yellow or red-skinned potatoes (about 12 ounces)

8 large eggs, lightly beaten

½ cup freshly grated Parmigiano-Reggiano

1¼ pounds asparagus, tough ends trimmed

Heat the oven to 400°F, with a rack in the middle.

For the aioli: Chop and smush together the garlic with the salt to form a paste. Transfer to a small bowl and stir in the remaining ingredients. Set aside.

For the frittata and asparagus: Bring a deep skillet or large wide pot of well-salted water to a boil. While the water heats, heat the oil in a large ovenproof skillet over medium-high heat. Add the chorizo, potatoes, and ¼ teaspoon salt and cook, stirring occasionally, until the potatoes are just tender, 4 to 6 minutes. Drain any excess oil. Reduce the heat to medium and pour in the eggs. Cook for 1 minute, then scatter the cheese on top. Transfer to the oven and bake until the frittata is set, 7 to 9 minutes.

Meanwhile, cook the asparagus in the boiling water until crisp-tender, 4 to 6 minutes; drain.

Using a spatula, slide the frittata onto a cutting board. Cut into wedges and serve hot or at room temperature, with the asparagus and aioli alongside.

Breakfast-for-Dinner PIZZA

with Eggs, Zucchini + Spicy Salami

Pizza night is super doable with store-bought dough (found in the refrigerator section of larger supermarkets). Eggs make a great topping for this one, and with the salami, it's kind of like a fancy egg sandwich. **SERVES 2 OR 3**

- 8 ounces fresh mozzarella, thinly sliced
- 1 (14-ounce) can whole peeled tomatoes, drained
- 1 tablespoon extra-virgin olive oil, plus more for brushing
- Kosher salt
- 1 pound store-bought white or whole wheat pizza dough, divided in half at room temperature
- All-purpose flour, for dusting
- 2 ounces sliced spicy salami, cut into strips
- 1 small zucchini, cut lengthwise into thin strips with a vegetable peeler
- ¼ cup plus 2 tablespoons grated Parmigiano-Reggiano cheese, plus more for serving
- 4 large eggs
- Grated lemon zest, fresh basil, or red pepper flakes or cracked black pepper for serving (optional)

Heat the oven to 500°F, with a rack in the lower third. Press the mozzarella slices between paper towels to remove excess moisture. Set aside.

Puree the tomatoes, oil, and ¼ teaspoon salt in a food processor or blender until smooth.

Place a cookie sheet in the oven to heat while you prepare the pizza. Cut a piece of parchment about 13 inches long. Put one piece of dough on the paper and, with lightly floured hands, stretch it into a rough 11- to 12-inch round or oblong. Spoon ⅓ cup of the tomato puree over the dough, leaving a narrow border all around. Arrange half of the salami on top, then top with half of the zucchini strips in a crisscross pattern and half of the mozzarella and Parm. Remove the cookie sheet from the oven and slide the pizza, still on the parchment, onto it. Return it to the oven.

Bake until the crust is just beginning to turn golden and the mozzarella is melted, 5 to 6 minutes. Crack 2 of the eggs on top of the pizza, season the eggs with a pinch of salt, and bake until the crust is golden and the egg whites are just set, 7 to 8 minutes more. Meanwhile, prepare a second pie with the remaining dough and toppings. (You will have leftover tomato puree.)

Remove the first pizza from the oven and slide it onto a cutting board. Brush the edges of the crust of the finished pizza with a little olive oil. Top with a sprinkling of Parm and a little grated lemon zest, basil, or red pepper flakes or cracked pepper, if desired. Bake the second pizza while you're enjoying the first. When the second one is ready, sprinkle with the toppings and serve.

EGG CURRY
with Green Beans

In little more than the time it takes to hard-boil eggs, you can have this aromatic South Indian-style curry on the table. Its rich base of tomatoes and coconut milk is seasoned with fresh ginger and garlic. Serve with steamed rice or your favorite flatbread (I like both). The optional yogurt topping adds a nice tang. The vegetable component is flexible—try spinach or cubed butternut squash in place of the green beans, if you like. **SERVES 4**

6 large eggs

2 tablespoons coconut oil

1 medium onion, finely chopped

1 medium jalapeño or serrano chile, cut lengthwise in half (seeds left in)

Kosher salt

⅓ pound green beans, trimmed and cut into 1- to 2-inch lengths

1 tablespoon finely chopped peeled fresh ginger

1 garlic clove, finely chopped

2 teaspoons curry powder

¼ teaspoon ground turmeric

⅛ teaspoon cayenne pepper

½ teaspoon grated lemon zest

1 (14-ounce) can crushed tomatoes

1 (14-ounce) can full-fat coconut milk, well shaken

1 tablespoon fresh lemon juice

Chopped fresh cilantro, plain whole-milk yogurt, and steamed long-grain rice or warm buttered pita, naan, or other flatbread for serving

Bring a medium saucepan of water to a gentle boil. Using a slotted spoon, carefully lower in the eggs and boil gently boil for 9 minutes. Transfer the eggs to a bowl of ice water and cool for 5 minutes, then drain.

Meanwhile, heat the oil in a large saucepan over medium-high heat. Add the onion, chile, and 1 teaspoon salt, reduce the heat to medium, and cook, stirring occasionally, until the onion is tender, about 5 minutes. Add the green beans, ginger, and garlic and cook for 2 minutes.

Stir in the spices and zest, add the tomatoes, coconut milk, and ½ cup water, and bring to a gentle simmer. Cook until the curry is thickened and the green beans are tender, 12 to 15 minutes. Remove from the heat, stir in the lemon juice, and adjust the seasonings to taste.

Drain the eggs, peel them, and cut them lengthwise in half. Add to the curry, then cover and let stand for 5 minutes to blend the flavors.

Serve the curry hot, topped with cilantro and yogurt and accompanied by rice or flatbread, as you like.

MY FAVORITE
SHAKSHUKA, PAGE 94

My Favorite Shakshuka

The Mediterranean skillet egg dish shakshuka is officially beloved, and for good reason. It's a filling dish made with simple pantry staples, and it's insanely good. It's also easy to vary and a cinch to make. And though it's on almost every restaurant brunch menu, it's not just for brunch! This version, made with ground lamb or beef, is especially hearty.

Vegetarians, please don't skip this recipe: Just leave out the meat. **SERVES 3 OR 4**

2 tablespoons extra-virgin olive oil

½ small onion, thinly sliced

1 small garlic clove, thinly sliced

Kosher salt

¼ teaspoon ground cumin

¼ teaspoon ground coriander

1 pound ground lamb

1 (28-ounce) can crushed tomatoes

½ cup coarsely chopped jarred roasted bell peppers (optional)

1 tablespoon harissa, or more to taste

½ teaspoon grated orange zest

6 large eggs

OPTIONAL FOR TOPPING AND SERVING

Plain Greek yogurt, crumbled feta, tahini, toasted pine nuts, thinly sliced fresh chiles, and/or chopped fresh mint, cilantro, and/or scallions

Warm pita or other bread

Heat the oil in a large skillet over medium heat until hot but not smoking. Add the onion, garlic, and ¾ teaspoon salt and cook, stirring occasionally, until the onion is just softened, about 3 minutes (do not brown). Stir in the spices, then add the lamb. Cook, stirring and breaking up the meat into small bits with a wooden spoon, until it is no longer pink, about 5 minutes. Pour off all but 1 tablespoon of the excess fat.

Add the tomatoes, red peppers, if using, harissa, and orange zest and bring to a simmer. Adjust the heat to maintain a simmer and cook, stirring, until the sauce thickens slightly, 7 to 9 minutes. Add more harissa, if you like.

Remove the pan from the heat. Using the back of a large spoon, make 6 little nests in the sauce. One at a time, crack each egg into a cup and gently tip it into one of the nests. Season the eggs with salt. Drag the edge of a spatula through the egg whites so they run into the sauce a little, being careful not to break the yolks (this will help the whites cook faster so the yolks won't overcook). Cover, return to the heat, and cook at a gentle simmer, gently basting the eggs occasionally with the sauce, until the egg whites are just set and the yolks are cooked to your liking, 8 to 10 minutes for runny to partially runny yolks.

Remove the pan from the heat, top the shakshuka as desired, and serve with bread, if you like.

See photo previous page

PORK & EGG
RICE BOWL
(KATSUDON),
PAGE 98

PORK + EGG Rice Bowl
(Katsudon)

Satisfaction made simple, by way of Japan. A sweet-salty broth animated with ginger and scallions and enriched with fluffy eggs smothers crisp pork cutlets. Called *katsudon,* the dish is a classic for a reason. Here it's served on a bed of rice. Who says Japanese food has to be difficult? **SERVES 4**

1½ cups jasmine or other long-grain rice

5 large eggs

⅓ cup all-purpose flour

1 cup panko (Japanese bread crumbs)

4 thin-cut boneless pork chops (about 4 ounces each)

Kosher salt and freshly ground black pepper

Canola oil for shallow-frying

2½ cups low-sodium chicken broth

¼ cup soy sauce

2 tablespoons rice vinegar

1 tablespoon sugar

1 small onion, thinly sliced

1½ tablespoons finely chopped peeled fresh ginger (from a 2-inch knob)

Thinly sliced scallions and (optional) red pepper flakes for serving

Cook the rice according to the package instructions.

Meanwhile, beat one of the eggs in a wide shallow bowl. Place the flour in a second wide shallow bowl and the panko in a third bowl.

Season the pork chops with salt and pepper, then dredge lightly in the flour. Dip one pork chop into the egg, then into the panko, pressing gently to adhere, and transfer to a plate. Repeat with the remaining cutlets.

Set a wire rack on a plate or small baking sheet. Heat ¾ inch of oil in a very large skillet or wide, heavy pot over medium-high heat until hot but not smoking. Fry the cutlets in batches, turning once, until golden and cooked through, about 3 minutes per side. Set on the wire rack to drain and cool, then slice crosswise into ½-inch-wide strips.

Meanwhile, carefully pour the frying oil into a heatproof bowl and let cool. Wipe out the skillet with a paper towel.

Whisk together the broth, soy sauce, vinegar, and sugar in a bowl until the sugar dissolves. In a second bowl, lightly beat the remaining 4 eggs with ¼ teaspoon salt.

Heat 1 tablespoon of the frying oil in the same skillet over medium heat. Add the onion and ginger and cook until softened, about 5 minutes. Add the broth mixture and bring to a simmer. Lay the pork strips in the skillet in a single layer, then drizzle with the beaten egg. Cover and cook until the egg is just barely set, about 3 minutes.

Spoon the rice into bowls. Top with the pork, broth, scallions, and red pepper flakes, if using, and serve.

See photo previous page

chapter four

SANDWICHES
+ their Cousins

I've *NEVER* met a burger I didn't like.

Croque Signore

Mortadella, the silky Italian sausage studded with little cubes of pork fat, might be my favorite deli meat of all time. In this Italian spin on the French melty ham and cheese sandwich called a croque monsieur, mortadella is paired up with pepperoncini and provolone. Serve with your favorite green salad alongside. **SERVES 4**

¼ cup unsalted shelled pistachios

BÉCHAMEL
4 tablespoons (½ stick) unsalted butter

¼ cup all-purpose flour

1½ cups whole milk

1 tablespoon Dijon mustard

¼ teaspoon kosher salt

Freshly ground black pepper

FOR ASSEMBLY
8 (½-inch-thick) slices rustic bread

6 ounces thinly sliced mortadella

8 ounces thinly sliced provolone cheese

⅓ cup chopped pepperoncini, plus more for serving

⅓ cup thinly sliced fresh basil leaves (optional, but I love)

1 teaspoon grated lemon zest

Heat the oven to 425°F. Line a baking sheet with parchment paper.

Spread the nuts on a small baking sheet and bake until fragrant and lightly toasted, about 5 minutes. Let cool, then coarsely chop.

For the béchamel: Melt the butter in a medium saucepan over medium heat. Add the flour and cook, stirring, until foamy and pale, about 3 minutes. Add the milk ¼ cup at a time, stirring constantly, until combined and smooth. Then continue cooking, stirring occasionally, until the sauce is thickened, about 4 minutes. Remove from the heat and whisk in the mustard, salt, and a generous grinding of pepper.

To assemble: Arrange the bread on a work surface and spread the slices evenly with the béchamel (about 3 tablespoons per slice). Arrange 4 of the slices on the prepared baking sheet, béchamel side up. Top with the mortadella. Continue building the sandwiches, using half of the cheese and all of the pepperoncini, pistachios, basil, if using, and lemon zest, then top with the remaining bread, béchamel side up. Top the sandwiches with the remaining cheese and season with pepper.

Bake the sandwiches until the tops are bubbling and golden, 12 to 15 minutes. Serve with extra pepperoncini alongside.

Oozy Egg + SAUSAGE SANDWICHES
with Melty Cheese + Giardiniera

While you can certainly serve this sandwich for breakfast, it's substantial enough for dinner. Giardiniera, sometimes called Italian mix, is a mélange of pickled vegetables that's sold in jars. It's great on all sorts of sandwiches, as well as burgers and even tacos. If you can't find it, use chopped pepperoncini or pickled banana peppers instead. If sandwich-size English muffins aren't available, go for standard ones and make smaller patties and more sandwiches. **SERVES 4**

1 pound sweet or spicy Italian sausages, casings removed

1 teaspoon smoked paprika

Kosher salt

½ cup mayonnaise

1 teaspoon Dijon mustard

1 tablespoon unsalted butter

4 large eggs

4 ounces young Manchego, Asiago, or sharp white cheddar cheese, thinly sliced

4 sandwich-size English muffins, split and lightly toasted (see headnote)

1 cup coarsely chopped drained giardiniera

2 cups loosely packed baby or torn arugula or mixed greens (optional, but I love)

Sriracha or hot sauce, such as Frank's RedHot (optional)

Mix together the sausage, paprika, and ¼ teaspoon salt in a bowl. Using damp hands, form the mixture into four ¼-inch-thick patties.

Stir together the mayonnaise and Dijon in a small bowl; set aside.

Heat a large cast-iron or nonstick skillet over medium-high heat until hot. Add the patties and cook until golden on the bottom, about 3 minutes, then turn and cook until cooked through, 2 to 3 minutes more. Transfer the patties to a plate and wipe out the skillet with a paper towel.

Add the butter to the skillet and heat over medium heat until it's melted and the foam subsides. One at a time, crack the eggs into the skillet and cook until the whites are set but the yolks are still runny and the edges are golden, 4 to 5 minutes; season with salt, then top with the cheese during the last 45 seconds to melt it. Remove the pan from the heat.

Spread half of the mayo mixture on the bottom muffin halves. Top with the sausage patties, eggs, giardiniera, arugula or greens, if using, and Sriracha or hot sauce, if desired. Spread the remaining mayo on the remaining muffin halves. Close the sandwiches and serve.

Curried Egg + Avocado TARTINES

Eggs get dressed for dinner in these pretty layered open-faced sandwiches. They're great when you're solo, yet special enough to serve to guests for a breezy meal. Boil the eggs and make the mayo ahead, if you have time—then it's only ten minutes to dinner from there. Toss together a salad to round out the meal.

Keep this recipe in your back pocket for parties too. Cut into small pieces, the tartines make a perfect cocktail snack. **SERVES 4**

8 large eggs

CURRIED MAYO
⅓ cup sour cream

⅓ cup mayonnaise

1 small garlic clove, finely chopped

1 tablespoon finely chopped fresh cilantro (optional)

½ teaspoon grated lemon zest

1 tablespoon fresh lemon juice

¼ teaspoon mild curry powder

¼ teaspoon kosher salt

⅛ teaspoon cayenne pepper

TARTINES
4 large slices sesame or other rustic bread, lightly toasted

1 avocado, halved, pitted, peeled, and thinly sliced

6 small or medium radishes, very thinly sliced

½ English cucumber, thinly sliced

Kosher salt and freshly ground black pepper

1½ loosely packed cups micro greens, mâche, or other tender baby greens (optional)

2 scallions, thinly sliced

Coarsely chopped fresh cilantro (optional)

Bring a medium saucepan of water to a boil. Carefully lower in the eggs and boil gently for 9 minutes. Transfer the eggs to a bowl of ice water and let stand for 5 minutes, then drain, peel, and cut into thin rounds. Set aside.

For the curried mayo: Stir together all the ingredients in a small bowl.

For the tartines: Spread 2 tablespoons of the mayo on each toast. Top with the avocado, radishes, cucumber, and eggs. Season with salt and pepper. Dollop with the remaining mayo. Top with the scallions, and more greens and cilantro, if using, and season with more pepper, if desired.

CHICKEN &
BEAN BURRITOS
WITH SPICY
PINEAPPLE
SLAW, PAGE 112

CHICKEN + BEAN
Burritos
with Spicy Pineapple Slaw

This burrito trades the usual rice for a cabbage and pineapple slaw, so it's lighter on the carbs but just as filling. Any sort of cabbage works well. Napa, aka Chinese cabbage, has feathery leaves that soften when dressed, while the sturdy leaves of the green variety hold their shape, so if you use regular green cabbage here, you'll have extra slaw; serve it on the side. Look for precut fresh pineapple to speed up your game.

Vegetarians can swap in chopped grilled zucchini strips for the chicken. **SERVES 4**

2 tablespoons plus 2 teaspoons extra-virgin olive oil

½ small onion, chopped

1 large garlic clove, thinly sliced

½ teaspoon chili powder

Kosher salt

2 (15-ounce) cans pinto or black beans, rinsed and drained

1 teaspoon grated lime zest

2 tablespoons fresh lime juice

6 cups thinly sliced/shredded napa or green cabbage

1½ cups cubed (¼-inch) pineapple (about 8 ounces)

1 large serrano or medium jalapeño chile, thinly sliced

⅔ cup coarsely chopped fresh cilantro

2 scallions, thinly sliced

2 cups shredded cooked chicken (about a third of a rotisserie chicken)

4 large (12-inch) or 6 (10-inch) flour tortillas

Hot sauce for serving (optional)

Heat the oven to 400°F, with a rack in the upper third.

Heat 2 tablespoons of the oil in a small saucepan over medium heat. Add the onion and garlic and cook, stirring occasionally, until softened, about 5 minutes. Add the chili powder and ½ teaspoon salt, then stir in the beans and cook until warmed through, about 5 minutes. Stir in the lime zest and juice and remove from the heat.

In a large bowl, toss together the cabbage, pineapple, chile, cilantro, scallions, remaining 2 teaspoons oil, and ½ teaspoon salt.

Place one-quarter of the bean mixture off center on each tortilla. Top each with one-quarter of the chicken and ½ to ¾ cup of the slaw. Roll up the burritos. Wrap each one in foil.

Arrange the burritos on a baking sheet and bake until heated through, 12 to 15 minutes. Serve with any remaining slaw on the side and hot sauce, if desired.

See photo previous page

Pork Burgers

with Gochujang Special Sauce

Gochujang is a sweet, spicy fermented Korean red chili paste that amps up these savory burgers. It's become so popular that you can now get it in many supermarkets, along with the kimchi. (Or order it online.) If you can't get it, Sriracha sauce, which offers a more garlicky flavor in place of gochujang's deep, rich umami, can be substituted. **SERVES 4**

GOCHUJANG SPECIAL SAUCE

½ cup mayonnaise

1 tablespoon gochujang (see headnote)

½ teaspoon grated lemon zest

1 tablespoon fresh lemon juice

1 tablespoon finely chopped scallion

¼ teaspoon smoked paprika

BURGERS

1½ pounds ground pork

1 scallion, thinly sliced

1 tablespoon finely chopped peeled fresh ginger

1 tablespoon toasted sesame oil, plus more for grilling

1 teaspoon kosher salt

½ teaspoon red pepper flakes

4 hamburger buns, preferably with sesame seeds, split and lightly toasted

Bibb lettuce leaves, kimchi, and/or sliced cucumbers for topping (optional)

For the special sauce: Stir all of the ingredients together in a small bowl.

For the burgers: Mix together the pork, scallion, ginger, sesame oil, salt, and red pepper flakes in a bowl. Using damp hands, form the mixture into four 1-inch-thick patties.

Heat a lightly oiled grill to medium-high or a grill pan over medium-high heat. Grill the burgers, turning once, until cooked through, about 4 minutes per side.

Assemble the warm burgers on the bottom buns, topping each one with the special sauce and lettuce, cucumber slices, and kimchi, if desired. Close the sandwiches and serve.

LAMB BURGERS
with Cilantro Chutney

These burgers were inspired by the fried lamb patties I fell in love with at Asma Khan's London restaurant Darjeeling Express. Tucking a little yogurt into the centers before cooking lends a tang that complements the richness of the meat. Be sure to seal the edges well to keep the yogurt inside.

If you're dairy-free, skip the yogurt. Peanuts or even cashews can be substituted for the almonds. **SERVES 4**

CHUTNEY

- **6 packed cups coarsely chopped cilantro leaves and stems (from 2 to 3 large bunches), rinsed and drained**
- **2 tablespoons unsalted roasted whole almonds**
- **1 large jalapeño chile, seeded, coarsely chopped**
- **1 teaspoon grated lime zest**
- **3 tablespoons fresh lime juice**
- **1¼ teaspoons sugar**
- **½ teaspoon salt**

BURGERS

- **1½ pounds ground lamb**
- **¼ cup finely chopped onion**
- **½ teaspoon ground cumin**
- **¼ teaspoon cayenne pepper**
- **Kosher salt**
- **½ cup plain whole-milk yogurt**
- **½ teaspoon olive oil**
- **4 pita breads, warmed and split, naan, or other flatbread**

OPTIONAL TOPPINGS

- **Sliced ripe tomatoes, chopped fresh mint and/or cilantro, thinly sliced scallions, and/or red pepper flakes**

For the chutney: Puree the cilantro, nuts, jalapeño, lime zest and juice, sugar, salt, and 2 tablespoons water in a blender until smooth. Adjust the seasonings to taste.

For the burgers: Line a baking sheet with parchment paper. Mix together the lamb, onion, cumin, cayenne, and ½ teaspoon salt in a bowl. Using damp hands, form the mixture into 8 patties, about 4 inches in diameter and ½ inch thick. Arrange 4 of the patties on the prepared baking sheet. Spread 2 tablespoons of the yogurt over the top of each, leaving a ½-inch border. Place the remaining patties on top. Using your fingers, pinch the edges to seal in the yogurt. (It's OK if a bit oozes out.)

Heat the oil in a large, heavy nonstick skillet. Working in batches, cook the burgers until the undersides are golden, about 5 minutes, then flip and continue cooking for 4 to 5 minutes for medium-rare. Keep warm.

Spread about half of the chutney inside the pitas or over the warm flatbreads. Tuck the burgers inside the pita or place on top of the flatbread, then top with tomatoes, mint, cilantro, scallions, and red pepper flakes, if desired. Drizzle with the remaining chutney.

ARMENIAN Pita Pizza

(LAHMAJOUN)

Big thanks to my Armenian Canadian friend Shant, who introduced me to this pita pizza (called *lahmajoun*) when we were students in Montreal. The sandwiches can be enjoyed rolled up, folded, or open-faced. Serve with a salad for dinner, or cut into small pieces for a party trick.

SERVES 4 TO 6

¾ cup coarsely chopped green bell pepper

¼ cup coarsely chopped onion

1 garlic clove, gently smashed and peeled

1 cup loosely packed fresh flat-leaf parsley leaves

½ cup loosely packed fresh mint leaves, plus more for serving (optional, but I love)

¾ pound ground lamb or beef, preferably lean

2 teaspoons tomato paste

¼ teaspoon ground allspice

¾ teaspoon kosher salt

¼ teaspoon freshly ground black pepper

6 (6-inch) pita breads

1 large tomato, finely chopped

OPTIONAL TOPPINGS

Plain tahini or tahini sauce (page 37), Greek yogurt, chopped fresh cilantro, thinly sliced radishes, sliced pepperoncini, and/ or chopped olives

Heat the oven to 375°F, with the racks in the middle and upper third.

Pulse the bell pepper, onion, garlic, parsley, and mint, if using, in a food processor until finely chopped. Add the lamb or beef, tomato paste, allspice, salt, and pepper and pulse two to three times to incorporate the spices. Transfer to a bowl and mix together with your hands to fully combine.

Spread the meat evenly over the pitas and arrange on two baking sheets. Bake until the pitas are warm and the meat is just cooked, 8 to 10 minutes.

Remove the pizzas from the oven and dab away any excess fat with a paper towel. Sprinkle with the tomato and additional mint, if using. Pass any additional toppings at the table. Serve open-faced, or roll up or eat pizza-style.

Polish BANH MI

This spin on the popular Vietnamese sandwich leans on smoky kielbasa in place of slow-cooked pork. A quick searing or grilling is all the cooking needed. Pâté is a classic banh mi ingredient that lends a creamy richness. Look for it at the cheese counter at larger supermarkets or at your local cheese shop. **SERVES 4**

QUICK PICKLES

2 medium carrots, peeled

½ English cucumber, halved lengthwise and thinly sliced

½ cup distilled white vinegar

⅓ cup sugar

¼ teaspoon kosher salt

SANDWICHES

1 teaspoon extra-virgin olive oil

1½ pounds kielbasa, cut into 4 pieces and each piece split lengthwise

4 small hero rolls, split, or 2 baguettes, cut into 4 (8-inch) lengths and split lengthwise (leave hinged)

⅔ cup mayonnaise

1 teaspoon soy sauce or tamari

6 ounces country pâté, thinly sliced

1 large jalapeño, thinly sliced

½ bunch cilantro, tough stems removed

½ cup loosely packed fresh mint leaves

Sriracha or hot sauce for serving

For the quick pickles: Using a sharp vegetable peeler, peel the carrots lengthwise into ribbons; or very thinly slice them. Combine the carrots and cucumber in a small bowl. Heat the vinegar, sugar, and salt in a small saucepan over medium heat, stirring, until the sugar dissolves, about 2 minutes. Pour over the carrot mixture and let stand until cool (and pickled), 25 to 30 minutes. (The pickles are best if used within 1 day but can be covered and refrigerated in their brine for up to 3 days.)

Meanwhile, for the sandwiches: Heat the oil in a large skillet over medium-high heat. Add the kielbasa, cut side down, and cook, turning once, until crisped and golden, 3 to 4 minutes per side. Remove from the heat.

Pull out and discard some of the bread from the interior of each roll or baguette half to leave a ¼- to ½-inch-thick shell. Spread the mayonnaise on both sides of each bread shell, then drizzle with the soy or tamari.

Drain the pickles. Layer the pâté, kielbasa, pickles, jalapeño, cilantro, and mint on the bottom halves of the rolls or bread. Top with hot sauce. Close the sandwiches and serve.

chapter five

CARB COMAS

I'm all for tradition, but I'm even more for **MESSING** with it. Learn the rules, then **BREAK** 'em. Now put on a pot of water.

Ben's Rigatoni alla Vodka with Chicken
129

Lemon Spaghetti with Toasted
Walnuts & Parsley
130

Farfalle with Almond-Basil Pesto & Zucchini
134

Whole Wheat Pasta with Sweet Potatoes,
Brown Butter & Sage
137

Pasta Carbonara with Peas
138

Penne with Fresh Tomato Sauce,
Burrata & Herbs
142

Baked Cheesy Mac & Broccoli
145

Creamy Pappardelle with Chicken & Bacon
146

Stuffed Shells with Turkey,
Smoked Mozz & Kale
150

BEN'S RIGATONI
ALLA VODKA WITH
CHICKEN · PAGE 128

BEN'S Rigatoni alla Vodka
with Chicken

I cook this dinner often for my best friend, Ben Levine. The sauce is usually finished with a splash of heavy cream, but yogurt gives it a livelier flavor and makes it a touch healthier as well. **SERVES 4 TO 6**

Kosher salt

2 tablespoons olive oil, plus more for serving

¾ cup finely chopped onion

2 garlic cloves, gently smashed and peeled

½ teaspoon red pepper flakes, plus more for serving

2 tablespoons tomato paste

1 (28-ounce) can crushed tomatoes

⅓ cup vodka

1 pound boneless, skinless chicken breasts, thinly sliced crosswise, longer pieces cut into halves or thirds

1 pound rigatoni or other short tubular pasta

1 cup loosely packed fresh basil leaves, any large leaves torn, plus more for serving (optional, but I love)

½ cup plain full-fat yogurt

½ cup freshly grated Parmigiano-Reggiano cheese, plus more for serving

Bring a large pot of well-salted water to a boil.

Meanwhile, heat the oil in a large skillet over medium-high heat. Add the onion and garlic and cook, stirring frequently, until the onion is tender, 6 to 8 minutes (do not brown). Add the red pepper flakes and cook for 10 seconds or so, then stir in the tomato paste and cook for 1 minute.

Add the tomatoes and ¼ teaspoon salt, bring to a simmer, and cook for 2 minutes. Stir in the vodka, return to a simmer, and cook for 5 minutes. Add the chicken and cook, stirring occasionally, until cooked through, 3 to 4 minutes. Remove from the heat and cover to keep warm.

Cook the pasta in the boiling water until al dente. When it's close to done, gently reheat the sauce if necessary.

Drain the pasta and return it to the pot. Stir in the sauce, basil, if using, yogurt, and Parmesan. Adjust the seasonings to taste. Spoon the pasta into bowls and drizzle with oil. Top with more cheese and some red pepper flakes. Serve immediately, topped with more basil, if using.

LEMON SPAGHETTI
with toasted walnuts + parsley

I turn to this traditional Italian pasta after long workdays when I don't feel like making a stop at the market, since I always have these ingredients on hand. My version makes the lemon more vibrant by skipping the usual cream. Walnuts add a nice crunchy texture. Swap them out for another nut or even toasted bread crumbs, if you like. **SERVES 4 TO 6**

Kosher salt

1 cup walnut halves

1 pound spaghetti

½ cup extra-virgin olive oil

2 garlic cloves, gently smashed and peeled

Grated zest of 1 large lemon

⅓ cup fresh lemon juice (from 2 lemons), or more to taste

½ teaspoon red pepper flakes (optional)

Freshly ground black pepper

½ cup finely chopped fresh flat-leaf parsley

Heat the oven to 350°F. Bring a large pot of well-salted water to a boil.

Meanwhile, spread the nuts on a baking sheet and bake until fragrant and lightly toasted, 10 to 12 minutes. Remove from the oven and let cool, then coarsely chop.

Cook the pasta in the boiling water until al dente.

Meanwhile, heat the oil in a small saucepan over low heat. Add the garlic and cook until fragrant and light golden, about 5 minutes. Remove from the heat. Stir in the lemon zest, lemon juice and, if you'd like a little heat, the red pepper flakes.

Reserving 1 cup of the pasta water, drain the pasta, then return it to the pot. Add the oil mixture, walnuts, parsley, 1½ teaspoons salt, ¼ teaspoon pepper, and ¾ cup of the pasta water and toss to combine. Adjust the seasonings to taste and add more pasta water if the pasta seems dry. If you like, add more lemon juice to taste. Serve immediately.

FARFALLE
WITH ALMOND-
BASIL PESTO
& ZUCCHINI,
PAGE 134

Farfalle

WITH

ALMOND-BASIL PESTO + ZUCCHINI

Thinly sliced zucchini becomes deliciously tender as it marinates in olive oil and lemon juice while you cook the pasta and buzz up the homemade pesto.

If your basil leaves taste bitter, soak them in ice water for 5 minutes, then drain (but don't dry) them before making the pesto. To save time, use ¾ cup (6 ounces) of store-bought pesto.

SERVES 4

PASTA

1 pound small or medium zucchini, sliced into very thin rounds (about 4 cups)

1 tablespoon extra-virgin olive oil

1½ teaspoons grated lemon zest

2 tablespoons fresh lemon juice

Kosher salt

8 ounces farfalle or other short pasta

¼ teaspoon red pepper flakes

PESTO

⅓ cup extra-virgin olive oil

3 tablespoons unsalted roasted almonds, plus more for serving

¼ small garlic clove

⅛ teaspoon kosher salt

4 cups loosely packed fresh basil leaves, plus more for serving

⅓ cup freshly grated Parmigiano-Reggiano cheese (generous ½ ounce), plus more for serving

For the pasta: Toss together the zucchini, oil, lemon zest and juice, and ⅛ teaspoon salt in a large bowl. Let sit for at least 25 minutes to marinate and soften while you make the pesto and cook the pasta. Bring a large pot of well-salted water to a boil.

For the pesto: Combine the oil, almonds, garlic, and salt in a blender. Puree until well combined and creamy. In 3 additions, add the basil leaves, blending just until pureed (do not overblend, or the basil will lose its fresh green color). Add the cheese and pulse 2 or 3 times just to combine. (The pesto can be made ahead; it will keep refrigerated for up to 3 days or frozen for up to 1 month.)

Cook the pasta in the boiling water until al dente. Reserving ½ cup of the pasta water, drain the pasta and transfer it to the bowl with the zucchini. Add the red pepper flakes, pesto, ¼ teaspoon salt, and a scant ¼ cup of the pasta water. Toss to combine. Add more pasta water to thin sauce, if necessary.

Divide the pasta among four bowls, top with the basil, cheese, and chopped almonds, and serve immediately.

See photo previous page

See photo previous page

CARB COMAS

135

WHOLE WHEAT Pasta

with Sweet Potatoes, Brown Butter + Sage

Making brown butter is a snap. You melt and then cook the butter over a medium flame. As the milk solids brown, a nutty fragrance fills the air. Toss in a few sage leaves, and about a minute later, you have a fancy-ish, rich sauce for whole wheat pasta.

If you see unsalted roasted hazelnuts at your market (try Trader Joe's), nab 'em and skip the toasting step. **SERVES 4 TO 6**

Kosher salt

½ cup hazelnuts (raw or unsalted roasted)

1½ pounds sweet potatoes (about 2 medium), peeled and cut into ⅓-inch cubes

1 tablespoon extra-virgin olive oil, plus more for serving

8 tablespoons (1 stick) unsalted butter

2 garlic cloves, gently smashed and peeled

Coarsely ground black pepper

1 pound whole wheat fettuccine

18 fresh sage leaves

1 cup (8 ounces) fresh whole-milk ricotta cheese

If using raw hazelnuts, heat the oven to 350°F, with a rack in the middle. Bring a large pot of well-salted water to a boil.

Spread the raw nuts on a small baking sheet and bake until fragrant, 10 to 12 minutes. Wrap the nuts in a clean kitchen towel and rub to remove most of the skins (it's OK if they don't all come off), then coarsely chop. Set aside.

Add the sweet potatoes to the boiling water and cook until just tender, 5 to 7 minutes. Using a slotted spoon, remove the sweet potatoes and drain well in a colander. Keep the water at a boil for the pasta.

Heat the oil and 1 tablespoon of the butter in a large skillet over medium-high heat until hot. Add the sweet potatoes, garlic, and ¼ teaspoon each salt and pepper and cook, stirring occasionally, until the potatoes are lightly golden, about 6 minutes. Remove and discard the garlic. Transfer the potatoes to a plate; set the skillet aside.

Cook the pasta in the boiling water until al dente.

Meanwhile, return the skillet to medium heat. Add the remaining 7 tablespoons butter and cook until melted. Continue cooking, swirling the pan occasionally and reducing the heat as necessary to prevent the butter from burning, until the foam subsides and the butter is golden brown and smells nutty, 3 to 4 minutes. Add the sage and cook until it is dark and crisp, about 1 minute. Remove the pan from the heat.

Reserving 1 cup of the pasta water, drain the pasta, then return it to the pot. Add the sweet potatoes, brown butter, and ½ cup of the pasta water. Toss to combine, adding more pasta water by the tablespoon if necessary to moisten the pasta. Adjust the seasonings to taste. Serve immediately, topped with dollops of the cheese, the hazelnuts, pepper to taste, and a drizzle of oil.

Pasta Carbonara WITH PEAS

Weeknight kitchen alchemy at its best: Hot spaghetti is tossed with bacon and beaten eggs, cooking the eggs and becoming a rich and creamy sauce in minutes. Grated zucchini and peas make the pasta a complete meal, so you can skip the side dish. **SERVES 4 TO 6**

Kosher salt

6 ounces thick-cut bacon, cut crosswise into ½-inch-wide pieces (about 1 cup)

4 large eggs

2 large egg yolks

1 pound spaghetti

2 cups frozen peas (no need to thaw)

1 medium zucchini, grated on the large holes of a box grater

1½ cups grated Parmigiano-Reggiano cheese (about 2¼ ounces), plus more for serving

1¼ teaspoons freshly ground black pepper

Bring a large pot of well-salted water to a boil. Meanwhile, cook the bacon in a large skillet over medium-high heat, stirring frequently, until the fat is rendered and the bacon is crispy just at the edges, about 5 minutes. Remove the bacon with a slotted spoon; reserve the drippings.

Beat the eggs and yolks in a bowl big enough to toss the pasta. Beating constantly, slowly add 2 tablespoons of the bacon drippings (if you don't have 2 tablespoons, just use what you have). Discard any remaining drippings.

Cook the pasta in the boiling water until al dente, tossing the peas into the water during the final minute. Reserving ½ cup of the pasta water, drain the pasta and peas.

Immediately add the pasta, peas, zucchini, and ¼ cup of the pasta water to the egg mixture and toss to coat. In 3 batches, add the cheese and toss. Add the pepper and ¾ teaspoon salt, tossing to combine. Add more pasta water as needed to loosen the sauce. Let the pasta stand for a minute or so to absorb the sauce, then adjust the seasonings to taste. Serve immediately, passing more cheese at the table.

PENNE WITH FRESH
TOMATO SAUCE,
BURRATA & HERBS,
PAGE 143

Penne
with
FRESH TOMATO SAUCE,
Burrata + Herbs

So quick and so easy, this dish plays on repeat in my kitchen during tomato season. While the pasta cooks, a sprinkling of salt helps the cherry tomatoes release their juices for a bright, fresh sauce.

Burrata is an Italian cow's-milk cheese made with fresh mozzarella and cream. If you can't find it, go for regular fresh mozzarella and, for a luxe, burrata-like effect, add a drizzle of heavy cream to each serving, if you like. **SERVES 4 TO 6**

Kosher salt

1 pound penne

2½ pounds cherry tomatoes, halved

¼ cup extra-virgin olive oil, plus more for serving

2 tablespoons finely chopped red onion

2 teaspoons red wine vinegar

1 teaspoon red pepper flakes, plus more (optional) for serving

1 pound burrata cheese (see headnote)

2 cups fresh basil leaves, torn if large

¼ cup finely chopped fresh chives or scallions

Coarsely ground black pepper

Bring a large pot of well-salted water to a boil. Add the pasta and cook until al dente.

Meanwhile, gently but thoroughly toss together the tomatoes, oil, onion, vinegar, red pepper flakes, and 1¼ teaspoons salt in a large bowl. Set aside.

Drain the pasta, then return it to the pot. Add the tomato mixture, making sure to scrape in every drop of juices from the bowl. Gently toss to combine well.

Divide the pasta among four to six bowls. Tear the cheese into pieces and place on top. Top with the basil and chives or scallions. Drizzle with oil, grind over some pepper, and add salt to taste and more red pepper flakes, if you'd like an extra kick of heat. Serve immediately.

See photo previous page

Baked CHEESY MAC + Broccoli

Broccoli and cheese make a great pair, especially in a baked pasta. You could substitute broccolini or broccoli rabe: Broccolini is slightly sweeter than broccoli, while broccoli rabe is pleasingly bitter. **SERVES 4**

Kosher salt

½ cup panko (Japanese bread crumbs)

2 tablespoons chopped fresh flat-leaf parsley (optional)

1 tablespoon chopped fresh thyme or ¼ teaspoon dried

½ teaspoon red pepper flakes

¾ cup freshly grated Parmigiano-Reggiano cheese

½ teaspoon grated lemon zest

4 tablespoons (½ stick) unsalted butter

8 ounces fusilli or other short pasta

1 large bunch broccoli (1½ pounds), trimmed, florets and stems finely chopped

2 tablespoons all-purpose flour

2½ cups whole milk

8 ounces mozzarella cheese, preferably fresh, torn into bite-size pieces (about 2 cups)

3 tablespoons fresh lemon juice

Heat the oven to 400°F. Bring a large pot of well-salted water to a boil.

Meanwhile, combine the panko, parsley, if using, thyme, red pepper flakes, ¼ cup of the Parmesan, the lemon zest, and ¼ teaspoon salt in a small bowl. Melt 2 tablespoons of the butter in a small skillet or in the microwave, pour it over the panko mixture, and toss to coat. Set aside.

Cook the pasta in the boiling water for 6 minutes. Add the broccoli and cook until it is crisp-tender and the pasta is al dente, about 2 minutes more. Drain the pasta and broccoli and set aside.

Add the remaining 2 tablespoons butter to the pot and melt over medium heat. Whisk in the flour and cook, whisking, until the mixture begins to bubble, about 1 minute. Gradually whisk in the milk, about ⅓ cup at a time, whisking until smooth between additions. Bring to a simmer, whisking, and cook, stirring occasionally, until the sauce is slightly thickened, about 5 minutes. Remove from the heat, add the mozzarella, the remaining ½ cup Parmesan, and 1 teaspoon salt, and whisk together until the cheese is mostly melted (the mozzarella may not fully incorporate into the sauce; this is okay).

Add the pasta, broccoli, and lemon juice to the sauce and toss to combine. Transfer to a large cast-iron skillet or 2-quart baking dish and top with the bread crumb mixture. Bake until the pasta is bubbling and the bread crumbs are golden brown, 15 to 20 minutes. Remove from the oven and let stand for 5 to 10 minutes to allow the sauce to thicken before serving.

CREAMY Pappardelle with Chicken + Bacon

This recipe recalls a classic Italian pasta sauced with braised rabbit, with rotisserie chicken (or any cooked chicken you have on hand) standing in for the rabbit. The chicken is folded into a rich, bacon-y cream sauce that drapes perfectly over pappardelle (or other wide noodles) for a comforting dish that's as good for a chilly night at home alone as it is for a casual yet special dinner with friends. **SERVES 4**

Kosher salt

8 ounces thick-cut bacon, cut crosswise into ½-inch-wide pieces (about 2 cups)

¾ cup finely chopped onion

2 garlic cloves, gently smashed and peeled

1 tablespoon plus 1 teaspoon coarsely chopped fresh rosemary or 1¼ teaspoons dried

Freshly ground black pepper

1½ cups heavy cream

2 (250-gram) packages imported pappardelle or other wide noodles

1 medium carrot, finely chopped

6 cups shredded rotisserie chicken, at room temperature

Freshly grated Parmigiano-Reggiano cheese for serving

Coarsely chopped fresh flat-leaf parsley for serving (optional)

Bring a large pot of well-salted water to a boil. Meanwhile, cook the bacon in a skillet large enough to hold the pasta and sauce or a wide heavy saucepan over medium-high heat, stirring frequently, until just cooked through with crispy edges, about 5 minutes. Using a slotted spoon, transfer the bacon to a plate, leaving the fat in the pan.

Add the onion, garlic, rosemary, and ¼ teaspoon pepper to the skillet and cook, stirring frequently, until the onion is tender, about 5 minutes (do not brown). Add the cream, bring to a simmer, and cook until the sauce is slightly thickened, about 5 minutes.

Meanwhile, add the pappardelle and carrots to the boiling water and cook until the pasta is al dente and the carrots are tender, 5 to 6 minutes. (If using other wide noodles, boil until al dente, adding the carrots 5 to 6 minutes before the pasta is done.) Reserving 1½ cups of the pasta water, drain the pasta and add it to the sauce, then add ¾ cup of the pasta water, the chicken, and the reserved bacon and toss to combine. Add more pasta water to loosen the sauce, if desired. Top with cheese, parsley, if using, and salt and pepper to taste. Serve immediately.

STUFFED SHELLS
WITH TURKEY,
SMOKED MOZZ &
KALE, PAGE 150

STUFFED SHELLS

with Turkey, Smoked Mozz + Kale

Using smoked mozzarella is one of my go-to ways to make an easy pasta dish taste complex. Since some shells inevitably tear or break during the boiling process, I usually cook the full box for this recipe. You can save the torn ones to toss with melted butter and herbs, if you like.

SERVES 4 TO 6

Kosher salt

25 jumbo pasta shells (from a 12-ounce box)

2 tablespoons extra-virgin olive oil

½ cup finely chopped onion

1 garlic clove, finely chopped

¼ teaspoon red pepper flakes

8 ounces ground turkey, preferably dark meat

5 ounces frozen kale or spinach, thawed, water squeezed out

1 cup (8 ounces) fresh ricotta

¾ cup coarsely chopped fresh basil, plus more for serving

1 large egg

8 ounces smoked mozzarella cheese, shredded

1 (25- to 26-ounce) jar marinara sauce (about 3 cups)

¾ cup freshly grated Parmigiano-Reggiano cheese (2 ounces)

Heat the oven to 450°F.

Bring a large pot of well-salted water to a boil. Add the shells and cook following the pre-bake timing on the package. Drain in a colander and rinse under cold water to cool. Set aside.

Meanwhile, heat the oil in a large skillet over medium-high heat. Add the onion and garlic and cook, stirring occasionally, until tender, about 5 minutes (do not brown). Stir in the red pepper flakes and ¾ teaspoon salt. Add the turkey and cook, breaking up the meat into very small pieces with a wooden spoon, until no longer pink, about 5 minutes. Stir in the kale or spinach. Remove from the heat.

Stir together the ricotta, basil, egg, and half of the mozzarella in a medium bowl. Stir in the turkey mixture.

Stir together 1 cup of the marinara and 3 tablespoons water and spread in a 9 by 13-inch baking dish. Fill the shells with the turkey mixture (about 2 tablespoons each), arranging them filling side up in the dish as you go. Spoon the remaining marinara evenly over the shells.

Cover the baking dish tightly with foil. Bake for 20 minutes, then remove the foil and top with the remaining mozzarella and the Parmesan. Continue baking, uncovered, until the cheese is melted and the sauce is bubbling, 10 to 12 minutes more. Top with extra basil, if desired, and serve.

See photo previous page

chapter six
Swim Team

Yep, I managed to make steamed MUSSELS POLISH.

SHRIMP
SAGANAKI,
PAGE 158

SHRIMP Saganaki

Crumbled feta adds a creamy, punchy bite to this quick-cooking Greek skillet supper of shrimp in a savory tomato sauce. Though the nuts, olives, lemon zest, and raisins are not traditional, they enhance the briny sweetness of the dish. **SERVES 4**

1 tablespoon plus 1 teaspoon pine nuts or chopped toasted almonds

2 tablespoons extra-virgin olive oil

¾ cup finely chopped onion

½ cup pitted Kalamata olives, coarsely chopped

⅓ cup raisins, preferably golden

1 tablespoon coarsely chopped fresh oregano or 1 teaspoon dried

¼ teaspoon red pepper flakes, plus more for serving

Kosher salt

1 (28-ounce) can crushed tomatoes

1½ pounds large shrimp, peeled and deveined

1½ teaspoons grated lemon zest (optional)

1 cup coarsely crumbled feta cheese (about 4½ ounces)

Lightly toasted rustic bread for serving

If using pine nuts, toast them in a large skillet over medium-low heat, shaking the pan occasionally, until lightly golden, 3 to 4 minutes; transfer to a plate and set aside.

Heat the oil in the same skillet (or a large skillet, if you didn't toast the nuts) over medium-high heat. Add the onion and cook, stirring frequently, until just tender, about 5 minutes (do not brown).

Stir in the olives, raisins, oregano, red pepper flakes, and ¼ teaspoon salt and cook for 1 minute, then add the tomatoes and bring to a simmer. Add the shrimp and lemon zest, if using, and cook, stirring occasionally, for 3 minutes. Gently stir in half of the cheese and cook just until the shrimp are opaque throughout, about 1 minute more. Remove from the heat.

Spoon the shrimp into bowls. Top with the nuts, the remaining cheese, and a pinch of red pepper flakes. Serve with bread.

GINGERY SHRIMP
+ GREENS SOUP,
PAGE 163

Gingery SHRIMP + Greens Soup

A box of stock, a bag of greens, and some shrimp: That's just about all you need to make this clean-tasting, gingery soup. White peppercorns offer a bright, sharp heat that works especially well with ginger. You can fall back on black peppercorns if you can't find the white ones, or use a mix. Cooked rice noodles can be added for a heartier dish. **SERVES 4**

2 quarts low-sodium chicken broth

1 (2-inch) piece fresh ginger, peeled and cut into thin matchsticks, plus 4 thin coins peeled ginger

3 garlic cloves, thinly sliced, plus 1 garlic clove, gently smashed and peeled

Kosher salt

1¼ pounds bok choy or baby bok choy, coarsely chopped

¼ cup canola oil

1 pound large shrimp, peeled and deveined

2 tablespoons fresh lemon juice

Toasted or hot sesame oil, and coarsely cracked white peppercorns or peppercorn mix, for serving

Combine the broth, ginger coins, smashed garlic, and ½ teaspoon salt in a medium saucepan and bring to a boil. Meanwhile, rinse the bok choy, leaving the water droplets on them. Set aside.

Remove the broth from the heat and cover to keep warm.

Heat 2 tablespoons of the oil in a large skillet over medium heat until hot but not smoking. Add the ginger matchsticks and garlic slices and cook, stirring constantly, until golden and tender, about 3 minutes. Add the shrimp and a generous pinch of salt. Cook, stirring occasionally, just until the shrimp are opaque throughout, 2 to 3 minutes. Using a slotted spoon, transfer the shrimp mixture to a bowl.

Add 1 tablespoon of the oil and half of the bok choy to the same skillet, increase the heat to medium-high, and cook, stirring occasionally, until crisp-tender, 3 to 5 minutes. Transfer to a bowl and repeat with the remaining oil and bok choy.

With a slotted spoon, remove the ginger coins and garlic from the broth and discard. Bring the broth just to a boil over medium-high heat, then remove from the heat and stir in the lemon juice. Adjust the salt to taste.

Arrange the shrimp and any juices from the bowl, and the bok choy in four large shallow bowls. Ladle the hot broth on top. Drizzle with sesame oil, sprinkle with cracked peppercorns to taste, and serve.

*See photo
previous page*

Shrimp + Chorizo "PAELLA"

The sweet juices of cherry tomatoes form the base of a saffron-y, garlicky sauce for shrimp and chorizo. The dish has the same satisfying appeal as paella, but with a shorter ingredient list and a simpler technique. Pearls of Israeli couscous stand in for rice. **SERVES 4**

2 cups low-sodium chicken broth or water

¼ cup extra-virgin olive oil

1⅓ cups Israeli (aka pearl) couscous

¼ teaspoon saffron threads

Kosher salt

4 ounces Spanish (cured) chorizo, thinly sliced

1½ pounds large or extra-large shrimp, peeled and deveined

1 garlic clove, thinly sliced

1 teaspoon grated lemon zest plus **1 tablespoon** fresh lemon juice

¼ teaspoon red pepper flakes, plus (optional) more for serving

1½ pints cherry tomatoes

½ cup loosely packed coarsely chopped fresh flat-leaf parsley, plus more for serving (optional)

Bring the broth or water just to a boil in a medium saucepan. Remove from the heat and cover to keep warm.

Heat 1 tablespoon of the oil in another medium saucepan over medium heat. Add the couscous and cook, stirring occasionally, until lightly toasted, 3 to 5 minutes. Stir in the saffron. Stir in the broth and ½ teaspoon salt and bring to a boil, then reduce the heat to low and maintain a simmer. Cover and cook until the couscous is tender, 12 to 15 minutes. Drain off any remaining liquid.

While the couscous is cooking, heat 2 tablespoons of the oil in a large skillet over medium-high heat. Add the chorizo and cook for 1 minute. Add the shrimp, garlic, lemon zest, red pepper flakes, and ⅛ teaspoon salt and cook until the shrimp are mostly opaque, about 4 minutes. Using a slotted spoon, transfer the mixture to a bowl.

Add the remaining 1 tablespoon oil to the skillet and heat until hot. Add the tomatoes with ¼ teaspoon salt and cook, stirring occasionally, until they burst and release their juices to form a sauce, 6 to 8 minutes. Add the shrimp mixture, parsley, if using, and lemon juice to the skillet and toss once or twice to finish cooking the shrimp and warm them through.

Serve the shrimp over the couscous, topped with more parsley, if using, and red pepper flakes, if desired.

SCALLOPS

with Burst Cherry Tomatoes

For this dinner update of a Porowski family summer rice salad, scallops are briefly seared in a skillet, and then tomatoes mingle with the glaze in the pan to form a sweet, jammy sauce. They're served over rice and corn, strewn with fresh mint.

Look for "dry-packed" scallops, which are not soaked in chemical preservatives. They're much tastier and easier to sear to a beautiful golden brown than their "wet" counterparts. Pull off the tiny rectangular bit of muscle from each scallop, because they are tough. **SERVES 4**

1 cup long-grain white rice

1½ cups fresh or frozen corn kernels

¼ cup plus ½ teaspoon extra-virgin olive oil, plus more for drizzling

Kosher salt

1 pound sea scallops, rinsed, patted dry, and tough side muscle removed (see headnote)

Freshly ground black pepper

2 pints cherry tomatoes

½ cup coarsely chopped fresh mint (optional, but I love)

Combine the rice, corn, ½ teaspoon of the oil, and 1 teaspoon salt in a medium saucepan, add the water specified on the rice package, and cook according to the package instructions.

Meanwhile, season the scallops with salt and pepper on both sides. Heat 1 tablespoon of the oil in a large nonstick skillet over medium-high heat until hot. Add the scallops and cook, undisturbed, until the undersides are deeply golden, 2 to 3 minutes, then turn and cook until just cooked through, 30 seconds to 1 minute more. Transfer the scallops to a plate.

Add the remaining 3 tablespoons oil to the skillet and heat until hot. Add the tomatoes, ¼ teaspoon salt, and pepper to taste and cook, stirring occasionally, until the tomatoes are golden, jammy, and burst, 7 to 9 minutes.

Divide the rice mixture among four plates. Top with the scallops and tomatoes, and then the mint, if using. Drizzle with oil, grind over more pepper, and serve.

MUSSELS
with Kielbasa + Horseradish Cream

Mussels are ideal for weeknight meals because they cook so quickly, and dinners with them are super riffable. I got the idea for this dish from Ed's Lobster Bar in New York City. I added cabbage and substituted kielbasa for the bacon in their version, and lo and behold, a Polish star was born. Serve with a stack of garlicky toasted bread to sop up the delectable sauce, if you like.

Choose refrigerated prepared horseradish for the best quality; shelf-stable kinds contain corn syrup, artificial flavorings, and preservatives. **SERVES 4**

4 pounds mussels

2 tablespoons extra-virgin olive oil, plus more for drizzling

8 ounces kielbasa, coarsely chopped

4 cups coarsely chopped green cabbage

¾ cup finely chopped onion

½ cup coarsely chopped fresh flat-leaf parsley, plus more for serving

3 tablespoons prepared horseradish

Kosher salt and freshly ground black pepper

½ cup dry white wine

⅓ cup heavy cream

Slices of rustic bread, toasted and rubbed with garlic, for serving (optional)

Rinse the mussels well under cold water. Pull off any beards and discard any mussels that are broken or gaping open.

Heat the oil in a wide heavy pot over medium-high heat until hot but not smoking. Add the kielbasa and cook, stirring occasionally, until crisp and golden, 3 to 5 minutes. Using a slotted spoon, transfer the kielbasa to a plate and set aside.

Add the cabbage and onion to the pot and cook, stirring frequently, until the cabbage is wilted and the onion is tender, 4 to 6 minutes.

Stir in the parsley, horseradish, ¼ teaspoon salt, and pepper to taste. Add the mussels, wine, and cream, increase the heat to high, cover, and cook, gently shaking the pot once or twice, until the mussels open, 3 to 5 minutes. Toss the mussels well with a wooden spoon, and discard any that have not opened. Stir in the kielbasa and cook for 30 seconds to warm through.

Spoon the mussels into bowls, then spoon the pan juices over the top. Drizzle with oil and sprinkle with parsley and salt. Serve immediately, with garlicky bread, if desired.

Salmon + Spinach RICE BOWL with Green Tea Broth

Gosh, I miss Japan. Never have I left a country so inspired by its cuisine and respect for simple food. At its most basic, this dish, known as *ochazuke,* is made by pouring hot green tea over rice. For a nourishing meal, I top the rice with broiled salmon (or arctic char) seasoned with sesame oil and then ladle over a tea and chicken broth blend. I prefer jasmine green tea, but you can use whatever green tea you like. **SERVES 4**

1 cup sushi rice or other short-grain rice

Kosher salt

1½ quarts low-sodium chicken broth

3 bags jasmine green tea, regular or decaf (see headnote)

1½ tablespoons soy sauce or tamari, plus more for serving

1⅓ pounds skin-on salmon or arctic char fillet

2 teaspoons toasted sesame oil, plus more for serving

1 bunch (8 ounces) spinach, tough stems removed, leaves and tender stems torn or coarsely chopped

2 scallions, thinly sliced

Toasted sesame seeds or torn roasted seaweed snacks or nori, for topping (optional)

Rinse the rice well in a fine-mesh sieve under cold water until the water runs clear. Transfer to a medium saucepan, add 1 cup water and ¼ teaspoon salt, and bring to a boil. Reduce the heat to the lowest setting, cover, and cook until the water is absorbed and the rice is tender, about 15 minutes. Remove from the heat and let stand, covered, for 10 minutes.

Meanwhile, bring the broth and ¾ teaspoon salt just to a boil in a small saucepan. Remove from the heat, add the tea bags, cover, and let steep for 5 minutes, then remove the tea bags, squeezing the excess liquid back into the pan (discard the bags). Add the soy sauce to the broth and cover to keep warm.

Heat the broiler, with a rack about 5 inches from the heat source. Place the salmon on a foil-lined baking sheet, brush with the sesame oil, and season with 1 teaspoon salt. Broil until the salmon is cooked to your liking, 5 to 8 minutes, depending on thickness. Remove from the oven and gently flake the fish with a fork. Discard the skin.

Divide the rice, salmon, spinach, and scallions among four large bowls. Bring the broth just to a boil and ladle it into the bowls. Drizzle with sesame oil and soy sauce to taste. Pass the sesame seeds and seaweed, if desired.

Broiled Fish + Asparagus
with Choose-your-Flavor Butter Sauce

This is one of my quickest, most delicious, fuss-free dinners. Since asparagus broils beautifully and quickly, it's often my side veg of choice for this meal. Serve a salad alongside or in its place, if you desire. Choose one of the four butters that follow—or make up your own. The flavored butters are also terrific for sautéed shrimp. **SERVES 4**

1 pound medium asparagus, trimmed

2 teaspoons extra-virgin olive oil

Kosher salt and freshly ground black pepper

4 (6-ounce) thin white fish fillets, such as hake, flounder, blackfish, or thin cod

Flavored Butter (recipes follow; choose one), still warm

Lemon or lime wedges for serving

Chopped fresh basil, cilantro, or mint for serving (optional)

Heat the broiler, with a rack about 5 inches from the heat source. Arrange the asparagus in a roasting pan or on a baking sheet, toss with the oil, and sprinkle with salt and pepper. Broil until golden and tender, 4 to 6 minutes, depending on thickness. Remove from the heat.

Meanwhile, place the fish on another baking sheet and season lightly with salt and pepper. Spoon the flavored butter over the fish.

Broil the fish just until it flakes with a fork, 4 to 5 minutes.

Serve the fish and asparagus with the pan juices, with citrus wedges alongside and fresh herbs strewn over the top, if desired.

Miso-Scallion Butter

4 tablespoons (½ stick) unsalted butter

1 tablespoon miso paste (any color)

1 scallion, thinly sliced

Melt the butter with the miso paste and scallion in a small saucepan over medium heat, stirring, about 1 minute. Transfer the butter to a bowl (use a rubber spatula to scrape all the good bits from the pan), then whisk well until combined (the mixture will come together as it cools a bit).

Spicy Mango Butter

4 tablespoons (½ stick) unsalted butter

⅓ cup diced fresh or thawed frozen mango

¼ teaspoon red pepper flakes

¼ teaspoon kosher salt

Melt the butter with the mango, red pepper flakes, and salt in a small saucepan over medium heat, stirring, about 1 minute. Remove from the heat.

Lemon-Tarragon Butter

4 tablespoons (½ stick) unsalted butter

2 teaspoons grated lemon zest

2 tablespoons chopped fresh tarragon

¼ teaspoon kosher salt

Melt the butter with the lemon zest, tarragon, and salt in a small saucepan over medium heat, stirring, about 1 minute. Remove from the heat.

Jalapeño-Lime Butter

4 tablespoons (½ stick) unsalted butter

1 large jalapeño, halved, seeded, and finely chopped

2 teaspoons grated lime zest

¼ teaspoon kosher salt

Melt the butter with the jalapeño, lime zest, and salt in a small saucepan over medium heat, stirring, about 1 minute. Remove from the heat.

Grilled SWORDFISH + SUMMER VEGS
with Citrusy Salt

A platter of grilled fish and vegetables is one of the easiest and quickest meals to prepare. Crush some fennel seeds together with salt, add a little citrus zest, and you've got a quick seasoning that elevates the dish. If you're not into fennel, swap in coriander, cumin, or mustard seeds, or any other whole spice that you like. The vegetables here are flexible; sliced raw bell pepper can be used in place of jarred, and any other fresh vegetable you like is fine. A grill basket or grid for the vegetables is handy if you're cooking on a wide-grated grill. **SERVES 4**

1 teaspoon fennel seeds

Kosher salt

½ teaspoon grated orange, lemon, or lime zest

Freshly ground black pepper

Extra-virgin olive oil for brushing

4 (6- to 8-ounce) swordfish steaks

2 medium red onions, cut into ¼-inch-thick rounds

2 small zucchini, cut lengthwise in half

1 medium eggplant, cut into ¼-inch-thick rounds

4 large jarred roasted red peppers, quartered lengthwise

½ cup fresh basil leaves, torn if large, for serving (optional, but I love)

Crush the fennel seeds on a cutting board with a heavy skillet. Add ½ teaspoon salt and crush with the fennel to blend. Transfer to a bowl. Add the citrus zest and a generous grinding of pepper, then blend the mix together with your fingers. Set aside.

Heat an outdoor grill to medium-high or heat a grill pan over medium-high heat, then brush with oil. Put the fish, onions, zucchini, and eggplant on a platter or baking sheet, brush with oil, and season with salt and pepper.

Grill the vegetables, turning once, until tender, 5 to 6 minutes per side. Transfer to a (clean) serving platter or individual plates.

Grill the steaks until the undersides are golden, 3 minutes, then turn and cook until opaque throughout, about 2 minutes more. Arrange on the platter or plates and add the roasted peppers.

Drizzle the fish and vegetables lightly with oil and sprinkle with the fennel salt. Top with the basil leaves, if using, and serve.

chapter seven

WINNER, WINNER
Chicken (+Turkey)
DINNERS

Poultry is the Meryl Streep of the protein world. From an elegant coq au Riesling to a simple rice bowl, it can play any part.

SHEET PAN
CHICKEN
WITH
ROSEMARY
& GRAPES,
PAGE 185

Sheet Pan Chicken

WITH ROSEMARY + GRAPES

Who doesn't love a great sheet pan recipe? The grapes burst as they cook, and their sweet juices mingle with woodsy rosemary and smoky ancho chile powder. I lean toward red grapes for their stunning color, but any sort will do.

Ancho chile powder (many supermarkets carry it), which is mild and raisiny, complements the grapes, but regular chili powder or any spice blend you like is good here too. Thyme or oregano can be used in place of rosemary. **SERVES 4**

2 medium red onions, trimmed, leaving some of the root end intact, and cut into ½-inch-thick wedges

3 cups red or green seedless grapes

10 rosemary sprigs

3 tablespoons extra-virgin olive oil

Kosher salt and freshly ground black pepper

4 whole chicken legs (drumstick and thigh; about 3 pounds)

1 tablespoon ancho chile powder or regular chili powder

2 tablespoons fresh lemon juice

Heat the oven to 450°F, with a rack in the middle. Line a baking sheet with parchment paper.

Arrange the onions, grapes, and rosemary on the prepared pan. Toss with 2 tablespoons of the oil and season with salt and pepper. Roast for 10 minutes.

Meanwhile, pat the chicken pieces dry, then season generously with salt, pepper, and the chile powder. Heat the remaining tablespoon of oil in a large skillet over medium-high heat until hot. Add half the chicken, skin side down, and cook until the undersides are deep golden brown, 3 to 5 minutes. Turn and cook for 1 minute more, then transfer to a plate. Repeat with the remaining chicken.

Transfer the chicken to the baking sheet, placing it skin side up and nestling it among the onions and grapes. Roast until the chicken is cooked through and the onions and grapes are tender and slightly caramelized, 25 to 30 minutes.

Drizzle the lemon juice over the chicken, onions, and grapes. Serve with the pan juices.

Vietnamese CHICKEN + RICE NOODLE Salad

With the crunch of fresh cucumber and cabbage, this salad is vibrant and healthy, and it's got just enough carbs to make you happy. A sweet-tangy Vietnamese-style dressing adds zing. Seed the chiles and cut away the inner ribs to minimize their heat, or leave them intact if you like it hot. **SERVES 4**

DRESSING
- 3 tablespoons fish sauce
- ⅓ cup fresh lime juice
- ½ garlic clove, grated or minced
- 1 teaspoon packed (light or dark) brown sugar

SALAD
- 6 ounces rice noodles
- 6 cups thinly sliced green cabbage (from a small head)
- 1½ tablespoons fresh lime juice
- 1½ tablespoons extra-virgin olive oil
- Kosher salt
- ⅓ cup roasted salted peanuts
- 1 teaspoon packed brown sugar (light or dark)
- 6 cups shredded rotisserie chicken or leftover chicken
- ½ English cucumber, thinly sliced
- 2 medium shallots, sliced
- 2 medium Fresno or jalapeño chiles, seeded if desired and thinly sliced
- 1½ cups loosely packed fresh cilantro, basil, or mint, or a mix
- 2 scallions, thinly sliced
- Lime wedges for serving

For the dressing: Whisk all of the ingredients in a bowl. Set aside.

For the salad: Cook the noodles according to the package instructions. Drain in a colander and rinse under cold running water; set aside.

Toss together the cabbage, lime juice, oil, and ½ teaspoon salt in a bowl. Adjust the seasonings to taste. Finely chop the peanuts with the sugar on a cutting board.

Arrange the noodles, cabbage salad, chicken, cucumber, shallots, and chiles on a platter or in individual bowls. Drizzle with the dressing. Top with the herbs, scallions, and peanut mixture. Squeeze the lime wedges over the top and serve.

Greek Egg-Lemon Soup with Turkey Meatballs

Addictively satisfying and soothing, this tangy, protein-packed soup, known as avgolemono, is rather like a lemony Campbell's cream of chicken, but more grown-up. It involves a cheffy trick that's easy to master: Beaten eggs are gradually warmed with hot broth (a process called tempering), just enough so you can then blend them into the soup and thicken it without scrambling. Reheat any leftover soup gently over a low flame to avoid curdling the eggs.

Shredded cooked chicken can be used instead if you want to skip the meatball step, or leave out the meat altogether for a lighter soup. **SERVES 4**

½ pound ground turkey

¼ cup chopped fresh dill, plus more for serving

1 scallion, thinly sliced, plus more for serving

1 teaspoon grated lemon zest

Kosher salt

4 large eggs, one separated

1 tablespoon olive oil, plus more for drizzling

2 quarts low-sodium chicken broth

1 cup orzo

¾ cup fresh lemon juice (from about 3 lemons)

Freshly ground black pepper

Mix together the turkey, dill, scallion, lemon zest, ¼ teaspoon salt, and the egg white (reserve the yolk) in a bowl. The mixture will be wet. With dampened hands, form the mixture into 18 loose, misshapen meatballs (they'll look more like dumplings), about 1 inch in diameter.

Heat the oil in a large nonstick skillet over medium-high heat. Add the meatballs and brown until golden and just cooked through, about 6 minutes. Remove from the heat and set aside.

Meanwhile, bring the broth to a boil in a large saucepan. Add the orzo with ½ teaspoon salt and cook until al dente, about 7 minutes. Remove from the heat and cover to keep warm.

In a medium bowl, beat the remaining 3 eggs plus the reserved yolk. Whisking constantly, beat in the lemon juice a little at a time to combine. Whisking constantly, slowly add about ¼ cup of the broth mixture, beating until well combined. Repeat twice, adding about ¾ cup broth in all, then whisk the broth-egg mixture into the broth in the pan. Add the meatballs and very gently simmer to warm through.

Season the soup to taste with salt and pepper. Serve topped with scallions, dill, and a drizzle of oil.

CHICKEN Paillards with Caper-Butter Sauce

This is the dish I tell friends on high-protein diets to order when we're at French or Italian restaurants. The time spent pounding the chicken breasts into thin cutlets (in French, *paillards*) makes them cook extra quickly and is well worth the effort. You can ask your butcher to cut chicken breasts into cutlets for you to save a step.

The buttery sauce, with its briny vinegar and capers, is the real highlight. If you don't have capers, try chopped olives instead. Making sure the butter is well chilled ensures a well-emulsified sauce. Serve with a crisp salad. **SERVES 4**

1½ pounds chicken cutlets or boneless, skinless chicken breasts

Kosher salt and freshly ground black pepper

2 teaspoons dried oregano

1 tablespoon extra-virgin olive oil, plus more if needed

¼ cup red wine vinegar

2 tablespoons capers, rinsed and patted dry

4 tablespoons (½ stick) cold unsalted butter, cut into small pieces

A chunk of Parmigiano-Reggiano cheese for serving (optional)

If you're using chicken breasts, use a sharp chef's knife to cut them horizontally in half. Place each chicken breast half or cutlet between two sheets of plastic wrap and, using a mallet, rolling pin, or wine bottle, pound to a ¼-inch thickness; remove the plastic wrap.

Season the chicken generously all over with salt, pepper, and the oregano, pressing the herbs on, if necessary, to help them adhere.

Heat 1 tablespoon of the oil in a large skillet over medium-high heat. Cook the chicken in batches, adding more oil if needed, until golden and cooked through, 2 to 3 minutes per side. Transfer the cooked pieces to individual plates or a large platter as you go. Reserve the pan juices in the skillet.

Add the vinegar to the skillet with the pan juices and bring to a simmer over medium heat. Add the capers, then add the cold butter, a few pieces at a time, whisking constantly. Remove the skillet from the heat and pour the warm pan sauce over the chicken. Shave Parm over the top, if desired, and serve.

Slow Cooker COQ au RIESLING

I've been making coq au vin since I first started cooking. Switching from the traditional red wine to Riesling, a white with orchard-fruit notes, and adding a touch of fresh tarragon will make you feel like you're living in the Alsatian countryside.

Rieslings are relatively inexpensive, but go for a mid-range bottle of a quality that you'd like to drink. **SERVES 4**

1 (4- to 4½-pound) pound chicken, cut into 8 pieces, back and neck reserved

Kosher salt and freshly ground black pepper

6 ounces thick-cut bacon, cut crosswise into 1-inch-wide pieces

8 ounces cremini or mixed wild mushrooms, stemmed if using shiitakes, caps halved or quartered if large

1½ cups (about 6 ounces) frozen pearl onions

2 medium carrots, cut crosswise into 2- to 3-inch lengths

2 garlic cloves, gently smashed and peeled

6 tarragon sprigs, leaves removed and reserved for serving, stems reserved

3 flat-leaf parsley sprigs, plus more for serving (optional)

1¾ cups dry Riesling or other dry, floral white wine

1 (14.5-ounce) can low-sodium chicken broth (1¾ cups)

3 tablespoons cornstarch

1 pound baby potatoes (about 1 inch in diameter) or larger red-skinned or yellow potatoes, cut into 1-inch chunks

3 tablespoons apple cider vinegar

1 tablespoon honey

Season the chicken generously all over with salt and pepper; set aside.

Cook the bacon in a large skillet over medium-high heat, stirring, until golden and crisp, 4 to 6 minutes. Using a slotted spoon, transfer to a slow cooker, leaving the bacon fat in the skillet. Working in batches, brown the chicken pieces (including the neck and back) all over in the bacon fat until deeply golden, 6 to 8 minutes.

Add the browned chicken to the slow cooker, along with the mushrooms, onions, carrots, garlic, tarragon stems, parsley sprigs, if using, wine, and broth. Cover and cook on low for 8 to 10 hours or on high for 5 to 7 hours.

Place the cornstarch in a small bowl. Open the slow cooker and transfer ½ cup of the cooking liquid to the bowl with the cornstarch, whisking to combine. Add the cornstarch mixture to the slow cooker, then add the potatoes, vinegar, and honey. Cover the slow cooker and cook on high for 1 hour more.

Remove and discard the tarragon stems, back, and neck. Adjust the seasonings to taste. Serve hot, topped with chopped tarragon and parsley, if using.

Chicken RICE BOWL

with Chili Mayo + Ginger

When I was a waiter at BondST, a fancy New York City sushi joint, I used to make a quick snack out of rice topped with pickled ginger and chili mayo. The combo was so addictive that I later added chicken and turned it into a meal. Look for pickled ginger in the Asian section of the supermarket. **SERVES 4**

1½ pounds boneless, skinless chicken breasts

1 (2-inch) knob ginger, peeled and cut into coins

1 teaspoon whole black peppercorns

2 bay leaves

Kosher salt

1½ cups long-grain white rice

¾ cup mayonnaise

2 teaspoons Sriracha, plus more for serving

¼ teaspoon toasted sesame oil

1 cup thinly sliced pickled ginger (from an 8-ounce jar)

4 scallions, thinly sliced

Place the chicken, ginger, peppercorns, bay leaves, 2 teaspoons salt, and 5 cups water in a medium saucepan and bring to a bare simmer over medium heat. (Don't try to speed the process by increasing the heat, or the chicken will be tough.) Reduce the heat to low and simmer until the chicken is cooked through, 10 to 12 minutes.

Meanwhile, prepare the rice according to the package instructions.

Transfer the chicken to a cutting board; set the poaching liquid aside. Let the chicken cool slightly, then shred it.

Stir together the mayonnaise, Sriracha, and sesame oil in a small bowl.

Divide the rice among four bowls. Spoon 2 to 3 tablespoons of the poaching broth over each serving, then top with the chicken, mayo, pickled ginger, and scallions. Finish with a little more Sriracha and serve.

YAKITORI CHICKEN
NIGHT, PAGE 198

Yakitori Chicken NIGHT

I learned about yakitori in Japan. The term refers to grilled chicken skewers, but at yakitori restaurants, vegetables are cooked the same way. The ingredients, which are often skewered separately, cook quickly, making this a great weeknight meal.

Bottled yakitori or teriyaki sauce can be substituted for the sauce below, but homemade tastes fresher and brighter. You can skewer the chicken and make the sauce up to 2 days in advance. Let them both come to room temperature while you skewer the vegetables.

Inexpensive bamboo skewers sold in packs of 100 can be purchased online and in hardware and kitchen stores. **SERVES 4**

SPICY MISO SOY SAUCE

½ cup soy sauce or tamari

1 tablespoon plus 1 teaspoon rice wine vinegar

1 tablespoon plus 1 teaspoon miso paste (any color)

1 tablespoon packed brown sugar (light or dark)

2 teaspoons Sriracha

1 small garlic clove, grated or minced

¾ teaspoon grated fresh ginger

YAKITORI

1½ pounds boneless, skinless chicken thighs, cut into 1-inch pieces

24 skewers, soaked in water for 1 hour if wooden or bamboo (unless using a grill pan)

3 medium zucchini (about 1 pound total), cut into ½-inch-thick rounds

8 scallions, cut into 1½-inch lengths

Vegetable oil for the grill

For the sauce: Combine all of the ingredients in a small saucepan. Bring to a simmer over medium heat and cook, whisking occasionally, until slightly thickened, about 7 minutes. Remove the sauce from the heat. Pour half into a bowl for serving.

Meanwhile, for the yakitori: Thread the chicken on eight of the skewers. Thread the zucchini, through the skin, on eight more skewers, using 3 or 4 pieces per skewer (push and turn the skewers slowly as you go so as not to break the zucchini rounds). Thread the scallion pieces onto the remaining eight skewers.

Heat a lightly oiled gas or charcoal grill to medium-high or heat an oiled grill pan over medium-high heat.

Place the chicken skewers on the grill or grill pan, brush with some of the sauce, and cook, turning once and brushing with sauce on the second side, until cooked through, about 6 minutes. Grill the vegetables (do not brush them with sauce), turning once, until charred and tender, about 6 minutes for the scallions and 8 to 10 minutes for the zucchini.

Serve with the reserved sauce on the side for dipping.

See photo previous page

TURKEY-STUFFED Poblanos

With a little sweetness and crunch from raisins and cashews, this dish offers a perfect balance of meat, cheese, and veg. If you have a choice at the market, choose rounder, squatter poblanos, which are a bit easier to stuff than long, skinny ones. **SERVES 4**

3 tablespoons olive oil

1 large onion, finely chopped

2 garlic cloves, finely chopped

Kosher salt

1 tablespoon plus 1 teaspoon chili powder

1 teaspoon ground cumin

1 tablespoon tomato paste

1 pound ground turkey, preferably dark meat

½ cup fresh or thawed frozen corn kernels

½ cup raisins

½ cup chopped salted roasted cashews

½ cup chopped fresh cilantro, plus more for serving

Freshly ground black pepper

8 ounces sharp cheddar cheese, coarsely grated (2 cups)

4 large poblano peppers (about 1 pound total), halved lengthwise and seeds removed

¼ cup sour cream

Grated zest and juice of 1 lime

Heat the oven to 425°F, with the racks in the upper and lower thirds.

Heat 2 tablespoons of the olive oil in a large skillet over medium-high heat. Add the onion, garlic, and ½ teaspoon salt and cook, stirring often, until the onion is softened, about 5 minutes. Add the chili powder, cumin, and tomato paste and cook, stirring, for 1 minute. Add the ground turkey and cook, breaking it up with a wooden spoon, until cooked through, 5 to 7 minutes.

Stir in the corn, raisins, cashews, cilantro, ½ teaspoon salt, and ¼ teaspoon pepper. Remove from the heat and let cool slightly, then fold in half of the cheese.

Arrange the peppers cut side up in a 9-by-13-inch baking dish. Drizzle with the remaining 1 tablespoon olive oil and season with ¼ teaspoon each salt and pepper. Divide the turkey mixture among the peppers, mounding it slightly if necessary. Pour ½ cup boiling water into the dish, around the peppers, and cover tightly with foil. Bake on the lower rack until the peppers are tender, 20 to 25 minutes.

While the peppers cook, whisk together the sour cream with the lime zest and juice and ¼ teaspoon salt.

Uncover the peppers and top with the remaining cheese. Turn the oven to broil.

Broil the peppers on the upper rack (or about 4 inches from the heat source) until the cheese is melted and bubbling, 1 to 2 minutes. Serve hot, drizzled with the sour cream and topped with more cilantro.

chapter eight

WE MEAT AGAIN

It's really all
about the
Condiments.

Strip Steak with Harissa Butter
& Parsley Salad
208

Charred Hamburger Steak with Wedge Salad
211

Turkish Meatballs with Eggplant & Feta
212

Vietnamese Pork Patties with
Sriracha Mayo & Broccolini
215

Slow Cooker Pork Carnitas
218

Smoky Bean & Sausage Ragout
220

Lamb Lollies with Mint Gremolata
223

STRIP STEAK WITH HARISSA BUTTER
& PARSLEY SALAD, PAGE 208

Strip Steak
with Harissa Butter + Parsley Salad

Melting a pat of good butter over a warm, juicy steak is the ticket to luxuriousness. Blend that butter with harissa, the North African chili paste (found in many supermarkets), and in two minutes, you've got an amped-up power player. Parsley is elevated from a forgettable garnish to the star ingredient of an accompanying salad. **SERVES 4**

STEAK

6 tablespoons (¾ stick) unsalted butter, softened

1½ teaspoons harissa paste

¼ teaspoon grated lemon zest

Kosher salt

2 (10- to 12-ounce boneless sirloin or New York strip steaks (1 to 1½ inches thick)

Freshly ground black pepper

2 tablespoons extra-virgin olive oil

PARSLEY-SCALLION SALAD

2 cups loosely packed fresh flat-leaf parsley leaves and tender stems

¼ cup thinly sliced scallions

2 teaspoons fresh lemon juice

2 teaspoons olive oil

Kosher salt

For the steak: Stir together the butter, harissa, lemon zest, and ⅛ teaspoon salt in a small bowl.

Season the steaks generously with salt and pepper. Heat the oil in a large cast-iron or other heavy skillet over medium-high heat. Add the steaks and cook, turning once, for 4 to 6 minutes per side, depending on thickness, for medium-rare (120° to 125°F, if using an instant-read thermometer). Transfer to a cutting board and let rest for 5 minutes.

Meanwhile, for the salad: Toss the parsley, scallions, lemon juice, and oil in a bowl. Season to taste with salt.

Slice the steaks and arrange on plates. Top with the butter. Serve with the parsley salad alongside.

Charred HAMBURGER STEAK with Wedge Salad

This is my at-home version of *svizzerina,* a simply seasoned hand-chopped hamburger steak from one of my favorite restaurants, Via Carota, in New York City. I make it with ground beef rather than hand-chopping the meat, with the same rosemary and garlic notes of the original. Mine has a radicchio wedge salad, but you can go retro and use iceberg lettuce instead. **SERVES 4**

MAYO
½ garlic clove

Kosher salt

¾ cup mayonnaise

½ teaspoon finely chopped fresh rosemary

DRESSING
½ cup plain whole-milk yogurt

2 tablespoons extra-virgin olive oil

1 tablespoon balsamic vinegar

¼ teaspoon freshly ground black pepper

HAMBURGER STEAKS
1½ pounds ground beef

1 large egg

1 tablespoon capers, rinsed, patted dry, and coarsely chopped

2 teaspoons Worcestershire sauce

2 teaspoons Dijon mustard

½ teaspoon kosher salt

¼ teaspoon freshly ground black pepper

1 tablespoon unsalted butter

SALAD
1 large head radicchio, quartered lengthwise and root ends trimmed (see headnote)

4 ounces blue cheese, crumbled (about 1 cup)

⅓ cup loosely packed fresh flat-leaf parsley leaves (optional)

For the mayo: Chop and smush together the garlic with ¼ teaspoon salt on a cutting board to form a paste. Transfer to a bowl and stir in the mayo and rosemary. Set aside.

For the dressing: Whisk together the ingredients in a bowl. Set aside.

For the hamburger steaks: Heat the oven to 200°F. Mix together the ground beef, egg, capers, Worcestershire, mustard, salt, and pepper in a bowl. Form the mixture into 4 patties, 4 inches in diameter and about 1 inch thick.

Heat a large cast-iron or other heavy skillet over high heat until very hot, 3 to 4 minutes. Add the butter and melt it. Add 2 of the patties and cook, basting occasionally with the pan juices, until golden brown, about 5 minutes on the first side and 1 minute on the second side for medium-rare. Transfer the burgers to a baking pan and keep warm in the oven while you cook the remaining patties.

For the salad and serving: Arrange the burgers on plates, with the radicchio wedges alongside. Spoon the dressing over the tops and in between the leaves of the wedges, then sprinkle with the cheese and parsley, if using. Serve the mayonnaise on the side.

Turkish Meatballs with Eggplant + Feta

If you've never broiled a meatball, this recipe could be a game-changer. The cooking time is quick; the meatballs brown well, getting crispy edges; and, unlike the skillet-cooked kind, there's no oily splatter. I serve them with little cubes of broiled eggplant on big romaine "boats," topped with feta and yogurt. They're just as good in tomato sauce over orzo, rice, or pasta on nights when you're craving carbs. **SERVES 4**

MEATBALLS AND EGGPLANT

1½ pounds ground beef or lamb, or a mix

1 large egg

¾ cup coarsely chopped dried dates, preferably Medjool (about 6 large)

¼ cup finely chopped onion

3 tablespoons pine nuts

¼ cup finely chopped fresh mint

1 teaspoon grated lemon zest

½ teaspoon ground cumin

¼ teaspoon ground coriander

⅛ teaspoon cayenne pepper

Kosher salt

1 pound eggplant, cut into 1-inch cubes

1½ teaspoons extra-virgin olive oil, plus more for drizzling

FETA-YOGURT TOPPING

½ cup plain whole-milk yogurt

Kosher salt

¾ teaspoon grated lemon zest

2 teaspoons finely chopped fresh mint

¼ teaspoon red pepper flakes, plus more (optional) for serving

8 ounces feta cheese, crumbled

1 head romaine lettuce, leaves separated

Heat the oven to broil, with a rack 6 to 8 inches from the heat source.

For the meatballs and eggplant: Mix together the ground beef and/or lamb, egg, dates, onion, nuts, mint, lemon zest, cumin, coriander, cayenne, and ½ teaspoon salt in a bowl. Form the mixture into 1½-inch balls and arrange on a baking sheet.

Broil the meatballs, shaking the pan to turn them halfway through, until golden and cooked, 7 to 9 minutes. Transfer to a plate and tent with foil to keep warm.

Put the eggplant on the same baking sheet, brush with the oil, and toss with ¼ teaspoon salt. Broil until tender and golden, about 7 minutes.

Meanwhile, for the topping: Mix together the yogurt, a pinch of salt, and 1 tablespoon water in a bowl. Gently stir in the lemon zest, mint, and red pepper flakes.

Arrange the lettuce on plates. Top with the meatballs and eggplant and season with salt. Top with the yogurt and more red pepper flakes, if desired, and the feta. Drizzle with oil and serve.

Vietnamese PORK PATTIES with Sriracha Mayo + Broccolini

Adding Asian ingredients to Italian sausage was something I did on a whim one night when I wanted to make a Vietnamese-y dish but only had Italian sausage to work with. Removing the sausage from its casing and adding ginger, scallions, and cilantro to it reframed the flavors of the meat, while its garlic and other base seasonings gave me extra bang for my flavor buck.

Use spicy or mild sausage, depending on your preference for heat. Broccoli can be subbed for broccolini. **SERVES 4**

SRIRACHA MAYO

½ cup mayonnaise

1½ teaspoons Sriracha

1 tablespoon plus 1 teaspoon fresh lime juice

1½ teaspoons fish sauce

¾ teaspoon sugar

PORK PATTIES

1½ pounds Italian sausage (spicy or sweet), removed from casings

½ cup finely chopped fresh cilantro and/or mint

3 scallions, thinly sliced

2 tablespoons finely chopped peeled fresh ginger

Finely grated zest of 1 large lime

Kosher salt

Vegetable oil for the grill pan

1 pound broccolini, trimmed, stalks cut crosswise into halves or thirds, any thicker stalks halved lengthwise

Lime wedges, steamed long-grain rice, such as jasmine, and (optional) toasted sesame seeds for serving

Bring a large pot of well-salted water to a boil.

Meanwhile, for the mayo: Stir together all the ingredients in a small bowl.

For the patties: Mix together the sausage, cilantro and/or mint, scallions, ginger, lime zest, and ¼ teaspoon salt in a large bow. Using damp hands, form the mixture into 12 patties, each about 2½ inches in diameter and ¼ inch thick. (You can cook a small bit of sausage in a pan to check the seasonings and adjust to taste if you want.)

Heat a grill pan over medium-high heat until hot but not smoking. Lightly brush the pan with oil. Add the patties and cook, undisturbed, until golden on the bottom, about 4 minutes, then flip and continue cooking until cooked through, 2 to 3 minutes more.

Meanwhile, cook the broccolini in the boiling water until just tender, 3 to 5 minutes; drain.

Arrange the rice, pork patties, broccolini, and lime wedges on plates. Drizzle with the mayo, sprinkle with the sesame seeds, if using, and serve.

SLOW COOKER
PORK CARNITAS,
PAGE 218

SLOW COOKER Pork Carnitas

Pork shoulder and the slow cooker are a match made in heaven. Heady with citrus and chile, the pork becomes deeply flavorful, succulently tender, and easy to shred after a long but totally unattended braise. Then all you need are a stack of warm tortillas, a heap of cilantro, maybe some crisp radish slices and/or shredded cabbage, chopped onion, and fresh lime (choose your favorites), and you have an impressive meal on your hands. Pass the hot sauce.

Any leftover pork (with its juices) freezes well. Heat with a can or two of pinto or black beans for a second tasty meal later on. **SERVES 6 TO 8**

6 navel oranges

4 large limes

1 (4- to 4½-pound) boneless pork shoulder (aka pork butt or Boston butt)

2 tablespoons dried oregano

2 tablespoons chili powder

1 teaspoon ground cumin

½ teaspoon ground cinnamon

2 large garlic cloves, grated or minced

Kosher salt

3 bay leaves

3 tablespoons finely chopped canned chipotle chiles in adobo, plus 2 teaspoons of the sauce from the can

FOR SERVING

Warm corn tortillas, thinly sliced radishes and/or shredded cabbage, chopped red or white onion, chopped fresh cilantro, lime wedges, and/or hot sauce

Grate the zest from 1 orange and 1 lime. Halve and juice enough of each fruit to yield 1½ cups orange juice and ½ cup lime juice.

With the tip of a paring knife, make about 25 X-shaped slits, each about ⅓ inch deep, all over the pork. Combine the citrus zests, oregano, chili powder, cumin, cinnamon, garlic, and 2 tablespoons salt in a bowl and work the ingredients together to make a paste. Rub the spice paste all over the pork and into the slits.

Place the pork, bay leaves, and chipotles and adobo sauce in a slow cooker. Add the citrus juices and stir to combine. Cover and cook on low for 8 to 10 hours or on high for 5 to 7 hours.

Transfer the pork to a cutting board, leaving the juices in the cooker, and let rest for 10 minutes, then shred the meat and place it in a bowl.

Season the pork with a splash or two of the cooking juices and salt to taste. Serve with any or all of the suggested accompaniments.

See photo previous page

Smoky Bean + Sausage Ragout

This quick, hearty recipe is a great one for busy days. It takes about 25 minutes, but tastes like it's been cooked for much longer. Enjoy it as is or over toast or buttered rye bread. **SERVES 4**

14 to 16 ounces kielbasa

2 tablespoons extra-virgin olive oil, plus more for drizzling

1 small onion, chopped

1 red bell pepper, cored, seeded, and chopped

2 garlic cloves, thinly sliced

½ teaspoon dried marjoram, herbes de Provence, or thyme

Kosher salt

Freshly ground black pepper

1 (28-ounce) can crushed tomatoes

2 (15-ounce) cans cannellini, great northern, white kidney, or butter beans

Chopped fresh flat-leaf parsley for serving (optional)

Cut the kielbasa into 3- to 4-inch lengths, then cut each piece in half lengthwise. Heat 1 tablespoon of the oil in a large skillet over medium-high heat. Add the sausage, cut side down, and cook until deeply golden and heated through, 5 to 7 minutes. Transfer to a cutting board.

Add the onion, bell pepper, garlic, and remaining 1 tablespoon oil to the skillet and cook, stirring frequently, until the vegetables are softened, 7 to 9 minutes.

Meanwhile, thinly slice half of the sausage.

Add the dried herbs, 1 teaspoon salt, and a generous pinch of pepper to the skillet and cook, stirring, for 1 minute. Stir in the tomatoes, beans, thinly sliced sausage, and ½ cup water, reduce the heat to low, and simmer for about 5 minutes to blend the flavors. Adjust the seasonings to taste.

Spoon the ragout into bowls. Drizzle with oil. Top with the reserved sausage, a grinding of pepper, and parsley, if using.

Lamb Lollies
with Mint Gremolata

Gremolata, a vibrant uncooked condiment made with fresh herbs, lemon zest, and garlic, is a dream addition to this simple but elegant dish. Make the chops for guests on a weeknight or enjoy a couple as something special for yourself after a long workday. Serve with green beans or asparagus. **SERVES 4**

GREMOLATA

½ cup coarsely chopped fresh mint

⅓ cup coarsely chopped fresh flat-leaf parsley

2 medium garlic cloves, thinly sliced

1 tablespoon grated lemon zest

LAMB

12 lamb rib chops (about 3 ounces each)

Kosher salt and freshly ground black pepper

Extra-virgin olive oil for brushing

Flaky sea salt, such as Maldon (optional)

For the gremolata: Finely chop together all the ingredients on a cutting board until combined.

For the lamb: Season the lamb chops all over with salt and pepper. Heat a large cast-iron skillet or grill pan over medium-high heat until very hot. Lightly brush with oil. Add the lamb chops in a single layer, without crowding (work in batches if necessary), and cook for 3 minutes on each side for medium-rare. Remove from the pan and let rest for 5 to 10 minutes.

Sprinkle the gremolata over the lamb, season with flaky salt, if using, or kosher salt, and serve.

chapter nine

COLD+ RAINY NIGHTS

Because some days
you just need
a HUG.

The Best Damn NACHOS

Nachos are my number one Tex-Mex indulgence. As a kid, I'd microwave a bag of tortilla chips layered with piles of cheese and scarf them down with an entire container of sour cream. Now I take a more professional approach, using powerhouse pantry staples like chipotles in adobo and pickled jalapeños to up the ante.

Store leftover chipotles in adobo in the freezer. **SERVES 4 TO 6**

3½ cups shredded rotisserie chicken or other cooked chicken

¾ teaspoon chili powder

¼ cup plus 3 table-spoons fresh lime juice (from 3 to 4 large limes)

2 tablespoons plus 1 teaspoon finely chopped canned chipotle chiles in adobo, mixed with 2 tablespoons of the sauce

Kosher salt

1 pound tomatoes, chopped (about 2 cups)

½ cup finely chopped red onion

3 tablespoons finely chopped seeded jalapeño chile

3 tablespoons chopped fresh cilantro, plus more for serving

1 (15-ounce) can pinto or black beans, rinsed and drained

1 (12-ounce) bag tortilla chips (thick ones, not the thinner type)

1 pound sharp cheddar cheese, coarsely grated

1 cup (8 ounces) sour cream

1 (4-ounce) can pickled jalapeños, drained

1 avocado, halved, pitted, peeled, and diced

Heat the oven to 425°F, with a rack in the upper third.

Stir together the chicken, chili powder, 3 tablespoons of the lime juice, 3 tablespoons of the chipotles and adobo, mixture, and ½ teaspoon salt in a bowl.

For the pico de gallo, stir together the tomatoes, onion, fresh jalapeño, cilantro, 1 tablespoon of the lime juice, and ¼ teaspoon salt in a second bowl.

Combine the beans, 1 tablespoon of the lime juice, and ¼ teaspoon salt in a third bowl and stir together, gently crushing the beans just enough to mix in the salt and lime juice and to keep them from rolling off the chips.

Arrange half of the chips on a baking sheet, followed by half of each of the following: chicken, pico de gallo, beans, and cheese. Repeat to make a second layer. Bake until the cheese is melted and golden, about 10 minutes.

Meanwhile, stir together the sour cream, the remaining 2 tablespoons lime juice, the remaining 4 teaspoons chipotles and adobo, and a pinch of salt.

Drizzle the nachos with the sour cream mixture. Top with the pickled jalapeños, avocado, and cilantro. Serve immediately.

OATMEAL PANCAKES
with Apples + Bacon

This breakfast-for-dinner is dedicated to one of my favorite humans and fellow food obsessives, my friend Gigi Hadid, who introduced me to oats in pancakes. I add fresh rosemary and a little black pepper to the sautéed apples that go on top, and then I dollop on the tangy, lightly sweetened sour cream that we Polish people put on literally every dessert.

As long as you have the oven on, go ahead and heat your plates. A warm plate keeps the pancakes hot and makes you feel good too. I like a smoky thick-cut bacon here, but use whatever type you prefer. **SERVES 4 TO 6**

SOUR CREAM TOPPING

1 cup (8 ounces) sour cream

¾ teaspoon sugar

¼ teaspoon vanilla extract

PANCAKES AND BACON

1½ cups all-purpose flour

¾ cup rolled oats

2 teaspoons baking powder

1 teaspoon sugar

½ teaspoon kosher salt

¼ teaspoon ground cinnamon

1½ cups whole milk

2 large eggs, lightly beaten

2 tablespoons vegetable oil, plus more for cooking

1½ teaspoons pure vanilla extract

12 ounces bacon, preferably thick-cut

APPLES

1½ tablespoons unsalted butter

2 Fuji or other crisp, juicy apples, halved, cored, and thinly sliced

½ teaspoon coarsely chopped fresh rosemary or ¼ teaspoon dried

⅛ teaspoon kosher salt

Maple syrup for serving

For the sour cream topping: Stir together all of the ingredients in a bowl. Refrigerate until ready to serve.

For the pancakes and bacon: Heat the oven to 200°F, with a baking sheet on the middle rack.

Whisk together the flour, oats, baking powder, sugar, salt, and cinnamon in a large bowl. Whisk together the milk, eggs, oil, and vanilla in a second bowl. Add wet ingredients and stir together to form a loose batter.

Heat a lightly greased large cast-iron or nonstick skillet or griddle over medium heat until hot. Scoop the batter by ¼-cupfuls onto the griddle, without crowding. Cook the pancakes until bubbles form on top and the bottoms are golden, 3 to 4 minutes, then flip and cook until the second side is golden, 1 to 2 minutes more. Transfer the pancakes to the baking sheet in the oven and loosely cover with foil to keep them warm while you cook the remaining batter.

Wipe out the pan and cook the bacon over medium heat until golden and crispy, about 5 minutes for thick-cut bacon.

Meanwhile, for the apples: Melt the butter in a large skillet over medium-high heat. Add the apples, rosemary, and salt and cook, stirring occasionally, until the apples are crisp-tender, 3 to 5 minutes. Remove from the heat.

Serve the pancakes and bacon warm, topped with the apples and sour cream. Pass maple syrup at the table.

Turkey Cheeseburger Soup

I make this soup as an offering to my seven-year-old self. With its silky cheddar broth, smoky seasoned meat, and tangy pickle-and-melted-cheese-toast topping, it says "cheeseburger" in the best way. **SERVES 4**

1 tablespoon extra-virgin olive oil

1 small onion

2 celery stalks, finely chopped

1 garlic clove, thinly sliced

½ teaspoon smoked paprika

¼ teaspoon ground cumin

⅛ teaspoon cayenne pepper

Kosher salt and freshly ground black pepper

1 pound ground turkey

1 tablespoon tomato paste

2 cups frozen peas (no need to thaw)

1 quart low-sodium chicken broth

3 tablespoons unsalted butter

3 tablespoons all-purpose flour

1 cup whole milk

3 cups grated sharp cheddar cheese (12 ounces), preferably orange

¼ cup sour cream

2 to 3 teaspoons Worcestershire sauce

3 tablespoons Dijon mustard

4 (½-inch-thick) slices rustic bread, cut to fit into your soup bowls

20 bread-and-butter pickles

Heat the oil in a wide heavy pot over medium heat. Add the onion, celery, and garlic and cook until softened, 7 to 9 minutes. Add the paprika, cumin, cayenne, ¾ teaspoon salt, and ¼ teaspoon black pepper and cook, stirring, for 1 minute. Add the turkey and cook, stirring and breaking it up with a wooden spoon, until cooked through, about 5 minutes. Stir in the tomato paste and cook, stirring, for 1 minute. Stir in the peas, add the broth, and bring just to a boil.

Meanwhile, melt the butter in a small saucepan over medium heat. Add the flour and a pinch of salt and cook, stirring constantly, until the mixture is slightly puffed, about 3 minutes.

Stir the flour mixture into the soup and simmer, stirring occasionally, until the soup is slightly thickened, 5 to 7 minutes. Stir in the milk and 2 cups of the cheese and cook, stirring, until the cheese is melted and incorporated, about 1 minute. Remove from the heat and stir in the sour cream and 2 table-spoons Worcestershire. Adjust the seasonings and Worcestershire to taste. Cover to keep warm.

Heat the broiler, with a rack 6 inches from the heat source. Spread the Dijon on the slices of bread. Top with the pickles, then top evenly with the remaining 1 cup cheese. Arrange on a baking sheet and broil until the cheese is melted and golden, 1 to 2 minutes.

Ladle the soup into soup bowls. Top each with a toast and serve.

Classic POLISH CABBAGE SOUP

In this soup, called *kapusniak* in Polish, I use cabbage in two forms: fresh and fermented (i.e., sauerkraut). The latter gives the dish its delicious tang. Serve with rye bread and cold butter, classic accompaniments. **SERVES 4 TO 6**

- 1 tablespoon extra-virgin olive oil
- 4 ounces thick-cut bacon, cut crosswise into ¾-inch-wide pieces
- 1 medium onion, coarsely chopped
- 1 garlic clove, thinly sliced
- 2 bay leaves
- ¾ teaspoon smoked sweet paprika, plus more for serving
- ½ teaspoon dried marjoram, herbes de Provence, or thyme
- Kosher salt

- 1 medium head green cabbage, cored and coarsely chopped
- 1 (28.5-ounce) jar sauerkraut (do not drain)
- 1 large russet potato, peeled and chopped
- 1 medium carrot, thinly sliced
- 1 medium parsnip, thinly sliced (or another carrot)
- 1 quart low-sodium beef broth
- Freshly ground white or black pepper
- ½ cup finely chopped fresh dill, plus more for serving

Heat the oil in a Dutch oven or other wide heavy pot over medium-high heat until hot. Add the bacon and cook, stirring frequently, until it is golden and most of the fat is rendered, about 5 minutes. Add the onion, garlic, bay leaves, paprika, dried herbs, and 1 teaspoon salt and cook, stirring occasionally, until the onion is tender, about 7 minutes (do not brown).

Add the cabbage and cook, stirring occasionally, until wilted, about 5 minutes. Stir in the sauerkraut with its juices, potato, carrot, parsnip, and ¼ teaspoon salt. Add 2 quarts water and the broth and bring the soup just to a boil, then reduce the heat to low and simmer until the vegetables are tender, 45 to 50 minutes.

Stir in the dill, season to taste with salt and pepper, and serve, topped with more dill, if desired.

French-Canadian BEANS + GREENS with Brown Bread

In late winter at Québec's *cabanes à sucre* (sugar shacks), French-Canadians turn maple sap into syrup. Some of the shacks have rustic dining rooms where hearty, classic fare, like baked beans, is offered. I tweak my stovetop version with Dijon mustard and of course use maple syrup, then slip in some greens for health. Swiss chard lends a mild earthy sweetness, but you can also use spinach, mustard greens, or kale. **SERVES 3 OR 4**

1 bunch Swiss chard

4 ounces smoked bacon, preferably thick-cut, coarsely chopped

1 tablespoon extra-virgin olive oil

1 medium onion, finely chopped

1 garlic clove, thinly sliced

Kosher salt

3 tablespoons tomato paste

2 (15-ounce) cans white beans, such as cannellini or navy, rinsed and drained

⅓ cup pure maple syrup

2 tablespoons packed brown sugar (light or dark)

1 tablespoon plus 1 teaspoon Dijon mustard

⅛ teaspoon cayenne pepper or red pepper flakes

Freshly ground black pepper

Thinly sliced dark brown bread and salty butter for serving

Trim the chard stems, then thinly slice. Chop the leaves. Rinse the leaves, leaving the water droplets on them. Set aside.

Cook the bacon in a large skillet over medium heat, stirring occasionally, until crisp, 7 to 9 minutes. Using a slotted spoon, transfer the bacon to a plate.

Add the oil to the same pan, then add the onion, garlic, and 1 teaspoon salt and cook, stirring occasionally, until the onion is softened, 5 to 7 minutes. Stir in the tomato paste and cook, stirring frequently, until fragrant, about 2 minutes. Add the chard stems and half of the leaves and cook, stirring, until they're just wilted enough that you can add the rest. Cook until all the chard leaves are slightly wilted, about 3 minutes more.

Add the beans, maple syrup, brown sugar, Dijon, cayenne, several grinds of black pepper, and 1 cup water and stir to combine. Bring to a boil, then reduce the heat to low and simmer, stirring occasionally, until the sauce has thickened, 12 to 15 minutes. Add a touch more water if necessary to loosen the sauce. Stir in the bacon. Adjust the seasonings to taste.

Generously butter the bread and arrange on plates. Spoon the beans over the top. Grind over some black pepper and serve.

Cheese FONDUE

with Lots of Good Things to Dip

The possibilities for what you can dip into cheese fondue are virtually endless. Cornichon pickles and slices of kielbasa (or prosciutto or ham) are my top go-tos, but the traditional hunks of baguette and some blanched broccoli and asparagus are just as welcome (as is a spoon, if I'm being honest). You can find many other good things to dip—including marinated artichoke hearts and Peppadew peppers—at supermarket olive bars. Also delicious: crisp apples or pear slices, sliced carrots, asparagus and endive spears, and pitted fresh cherries.

A fondue pot and those long forks for dipping are useful for the full French/Swiss communal experience, but in a pinch, you and your friends can just gather around the stove with everyday flatware at the ready. **SERVES 4**

1 pound Gruyère, Emmenthaler, or Comté cheese, or a mix, coarsely grated (4 cups)

2 teaspoons cornstarch

¼ teaspoon freshly grated nutmeg

1 garlic clove, halved

⅔ cup dry Riesling or other dry, floral white wine

1 tablespoon fresh lemon juice

Freshly ground black pepper

CHOICE OF DIPPING STUFF
(see headnote)

Toss together the cheese, cornstarch, and nutmeg in a bowl. Rub the inside of a heavy medium saucepan with the cut sides of the garlic clove; discard the garlic. Add the wine to the pan and bring just to a simmer over medium heat.

Gradually add the cheese in ⅓- to ½-cupfuls, stirring constantly back and forth across the pan rather than in a circular motion to prevent the cheese from clumping up. Reduce the heat if necessary to maintain a simmer. Once all the cheese has been added, simmer, stirring, for 2 minutes to ensure it is well incorporated. Stir in the lemon juice and season with pepper. Serve immediately with your choice of good stuff for dipping.

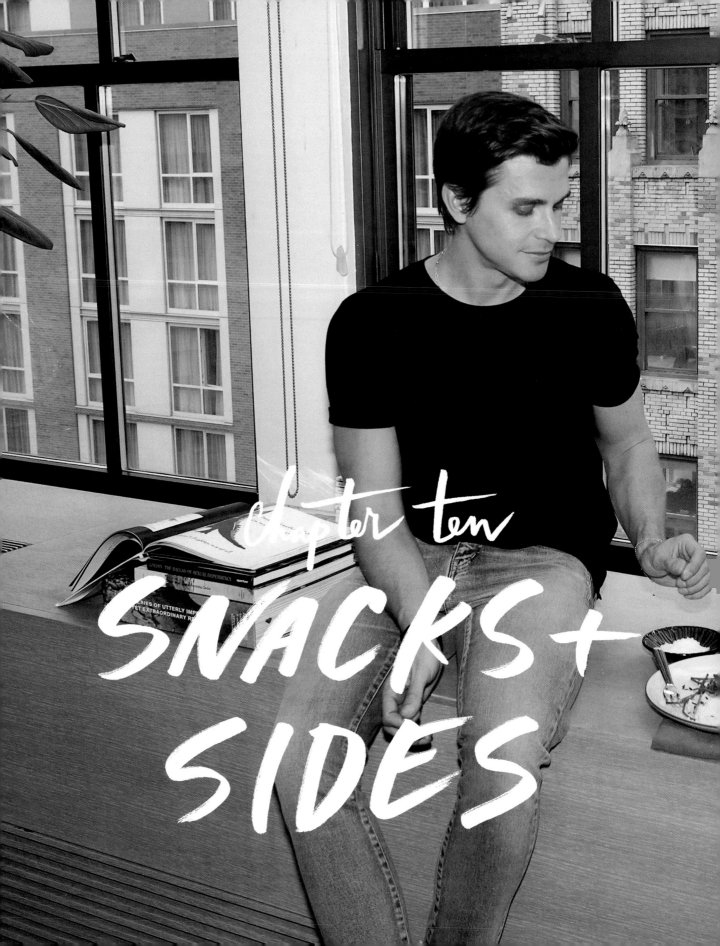

chapter ten

SNACKS+
SIDES

Different enough
but still familiar,
like parting your hair
the other way for a change.

Mashed Potatoes with Fries
245

Mortadella Fries with Honey Mustard
246

Crispy Smashed Potatoes
249

Old Bay Sweet Potato Wedges
250

Sweet Chili Brussels Sprouts & Chorizo
253

Ginger-Curry Glazed Carrots
254

Buffalo Cauliflower Fritters
257

Roasted Leeks with Black Pepper & Parm
258

Celery with Lemon & Anchovy Butter
261

Baked Zucchini with Cheesy
Garlic Bread Crumbs
262

Mashed Potatoes with FRIES

"A Tale of Two Potatoes." "Excessive." "Superfluous." "Redundant." That's how my friend Patti Felker describes this crazy-delicious dish, in which silky mashed potatoes become a dip for crisp shoestring fries. Crispy and creamy all at once, it's totally great as a Sunday-night special on your couch. Gigi Hadid agrees; she introduced it to me at L'Avenue restaurant in New York City.

A potato ricer is an inexpensive, handy tool that's important here (a food mill is also great). If you don't have either, use the back of a spoon to push the potatoes through the holes of a colander for a similar effect. Sorry, but no: You can't mash the potatoes with an electric mixer, or they'll be dense and gluey, not light as air. **SERVES 2 TO 4**

MASHED POTATOES
1 pound russet potatoes, peeled and cut into 1-inch pieces

Kosher salt

3 tablespoons unsalted butter, cut into chunks

½ cup sour cream

½ cup whole milk

FRIES
1 pound russet potatoes

1 to 1½ quarts canola oil

Kosher salt

2 tablespoons chopped fresh chives or scallions

Flaky sea salt, such as Maldon (optional)

For the mashed potatoes: Place the potatoes and 2 tablespoons salt in a medium pot and add enough cold water to cover by 1 inch. Bring to a boil and cook until the potatoes are very tender, about 10 minutes. Drain, return to the pot, and turn the heat to low just to dry the potatoes.

Pass the potatoes through a ricer (see headnote) and return them to the pot. Add the butter, sour cream, milk, and a pinch of salt and stir over low heat just to combine. Adjust the seasoning to taste. Remove the pot from the heat, cover, and set aside.

For the fries: Using a chef's knife or a mandoline slicer, cut the potatoes lengthwise into ⅛-inch-thick slices. Pat the slices dry with paper towels. With a knife, cut them on the bias into skinny sticks. Pat the potato sticks dry.

Line a baking sheet with paper towels. Heat 2 inches of oil in a deep heavy pot over medium heat until it shimmers—325°F on a deep-fry thermometer, if you have one. If you don't have a thermometer, test the oil by dipping in the tip of a chopstick or the handle of a wooden spoon; if the oil bubbles around it, reduce the heat a bit. Working in batches to avoid crowding, fry the potatoes until golden brown, about 5 minutes per batch (return the oil to 325°F between batches). Using a slotted spoon, transfer the fries to the prepared baking sheet to drain, and season with salt.

Warm the mashed potatoes over low heat or in the microwave, then spread them on a platter or plates and top with the fries. Top with the chives or scallions and season with flaky salt to taste. Serve immediately.

Mortadella FRIES with Honey Mustard

When mortadella (aka fancy Italian bologna) is cut into French fry-like strips, crisped in a skillet, and slathered in honey mustard, it becomes a ketotarian's dream junk food. Ask your deli person to slice the mortadella. **SERVES 4**

3 tablespoons Dijon mustard

3 tablespoons honey

¼ teaspoon cayenne pepper

2 tablespoons extra-virgin olive oil

1 pound mortadella sliced ¼ inch thick, cut into 3-inch-long sticks

Cornichon pickles for serving

Mix together the mustard, honey, and cayenne in a small bowl.

Line a large plate with paper towels. Heat 1 tablespoon of the oil in a large nonstick skillet over medium-high heat until hot but not smoking. Add half of the mortadella sticks and cook, turning occasionally, until browned on all sides, about 4 minutes. Drain on the paper towels. Repeat with the remaining oil and mortadella.

Transfer the fried mortadella to a platter. Serve with the honey mustard and pickles.

CRISPY Smashed Potatoes

While these taters take a bit of time, it's mostly hands-off and totally fuss-free. Flattening the boiled potatoes before roasting creates cracks and ridges that become perfectly crisp as they cook. **SERVES 4**

2 pounds small (1½ to 2 inches in diameter) red-skinned or white potatoes

Kosher salt

2 tablespoons extra-virgin olive oil

Freshly ground black pepper

Heat the oven to 450°F, with a rack in the middle. Line a baking sheet with parchment paper.

Put the potatoes in a medium saucepan, cover with cold water, add 1 tablespoon salt, and bring to boil, then cover and simmer until the potatoes are just tender, 15 to 20 minutes. Drain, then transfer the potatoes to the prepared baking sheet. Let stand until cool enough to handle.

Using the heel of your hand, gently smash each potato to ½ inch thick. Brush or drizzle the potatoes with the oil and season generously with salt and pepper. Roast until the edges are deeply golden and crisp, 35 to 40 minutes. Serve hot.

Old Bay Sweet Potato Wedges

A masterful blend of many of my favorite seasonings—celery salt, paprika, and cayenne—gives an all-in-one flavor boost to these tender baked sweets. **SERVES 4**

2 pounds sweet potatoes, cut lengthwise into 8 wedges each

3 tablespoons extra-virgin olive oil

2 teaspoons Old Bay seasoning, plus more for serving

Chopped fresh flat-leaf parsley for serving (optional)

Heat the oven to 450°F, with the racks in the middle and upper third. Heat two large baking sheets (not nonstick) in the oven for 10 minutes.

Toss the sweet potatoes with the oil and Old Bay in a large bowl. Spread the sweet potatoes on the hot baking sheets in a single layer.

Roast the potatoes, rotating the baking sheets and switching their positions on the racks once halfway through, until tender and golden, about 25 minutes. Season with more Old Bay to taste and sprinkle with parsley, if using. Serve hot.

SWEET CHILI Brussels Sprouts + CHORIZO

As if crispy roasted Brussels weren't great enough on their own, along comes a dynamic duo— sweet chili sauce and garlicky, smoky chorizo—to make them the best thing ever. **SERVES 4**

1½ pounds Brussels sprouts, trimmed and halved

3 tablespoons extra-virgin olive oil

½ teaspoon kosher salt

½ teaspoon red pepper flakes

3 ounces Spanish (cured) chorizo, chopped (about ¾ cup)

⅓ cup Asian sweet chili sauce

¼ cup chopped fresh cilantro (optional)

Heat the oven to 450°F, with a rack in the lower third. Set a baking sheet on the rack to heat.

Toss together the Brussels sprouts, oil, salt, and red pepper flakes in a bowl. Arrange the Brussels sprouts on the hot baking sheet in a single layer. Roast for 25 minutes.

Add the chorizo and chili sauce to the Brussels sprouts and stir to combine well. Shake the pan to return the Brussels sprouts to an even layer. Continue roasting until the sprouts are crispy, about 10 minutes more. Serve hot, topped with the cilantro, if desired.

Ginger-Curry Glazed Carrots

Curry powder, ginger, and citrus give classic glazed carrot coins a new dimension. You can use scallion greens or chives in place of the cilantro, or leave out the herbs altogether. Since carrot (and other fruit and veg) peels are nutrient-rich, I generally leave them on. **SERVES 4**

1½ pounds medium carrots, cut into ¼-inch-thick coins

3 tablespoons unsalted butter, cut into small cubes

3 tablespoons fresh orange juice

3 tablespoons honey

2 tablespoons finely chopped fresh cilantro (see headnote), plus more for serving (optional)

1 tablespoon finely chopped peeled fresh ginger

1 teaspoon grated lemon zest

½ teaspoon curry powder

Kosher salt

1 tablespoon fresh lemon juice

Pinch of cayenne pepper

Combine the carrots, butter, orange juice, honey, cilantro, if using, ginger, lemon zest, curry powder, and ½ teaspoon salt in a large skillet or wide heavy pot. Cover and cook over medium heat until the carrots are crisp-tender, 10 to 12 minutes.

Uncover and continue to cook, stirring occasionally, until the liquid thickens enough to coat the carrots, 8 to 10 minutes. Remove from the heat and stir in the lemon juice and cayenne. Adjust the seasonings to taste, top with more cilantro, if using, and serve.

BUFFALO
Cauliflower FRITTERS

This recipe is dedicated to my good pal journalist Sam Lansky, who shares my love for fried cauliflower covered in spicy Buffalo sauce. The sauce, made with yogurt instead of the usual sour cream and heavy cream, is still satisfyingly decadent, and a great foil for the salty, crisp fritters.

Using chickpea flour will make the dish gluten free; Bob's Red Mill, found in many supermarkets, is a reliable brand. **SERVES 4**

BUFFALO SAUCE

- 1 cup (8 ounces) plain Greek yogurt
- ⅔ cup crumbled blue cheese
- 2 tablespoons mayonnaise
- 4 teaspoons hot sauce, such as Frank's RedHot, plus (optional) more for serving
- 1 teaspoon fresh lemon juice

FRITTERS

- 4 cups coarsely chopped cauliflower florets, stalk, and stems (about 1 pound)
- 4 large eggs
- ¼ cup chickpea flour or all-purpose flour
- 4 scallions, thinly sliced (about ¾ cup), plus more for serving
- 1 garlic clove, finely chopped
- ¼ teaspoon cayenne pepper
- Kosher salt
- Extra-virgin olive oil for shallow-frying

Heat the oven to 200°F. Line a baking sheet or large ovenproof plate with paper towels.

For the Buffalo sauce: Mix together the yogurt, cheese, mayo, 1 tablespoon water, hot sauce, and lemon juice in a bowl. Cover and refrigerate.

For the fritters: In two batches, pulse the cauliflower pieces in a food processor until chopped into small pieces that resemble rice. Lightly beat the eggs in a large bowl. Add the riced cauliflower, flour, scallions, garlic, cayenne, and ½ teaspoon salt and stir together to form a thick pancake-like batter.

Heat 1 tablespoon oil in a large skillet over medium-high heat until hot but not smoking. Working in batches, scoop ¼-cupfuls of the batter into the skillet, without crowding, then use the back of the scoop to flatten each fritter to ⅛ inch thick. Cook until the tops bubble and appear dry and the bottoms are golden, about 4 minutes, then turn and continue cooking until the undersides are golden, about 3 minutes more. Transfer the fritters to the prepared baking sheet or plate, season with salt, and keep warm in the oven while you fry the remaining fritters.

Serve warm, topped with more scallions, the Buffalo sauce, and with extra hot sauce, if desired.

Roasted LEEKS with Black Pepper + Parm

Leeks become melty and sweet when roasted. A sprinkling of Parm and black pepper makes them even more appealing. Some nights I top these with a fried egg and call it a meal. On others, I serve them beside roasted, grilled, or pan-seared meat or fish or in a lineup of other veggie dishes. **SERVES 4**

¼ cup extra-virgin olive oil

2 tablespoons finely chopped fresh soft herbs, such as tarragon, marjoram, chives, and/or basil, plus more for serving

1 tablespoon Dijon mustard

¼ teaspoon grated lemon zest

½ teaspoon fresh lemon juice, plus 1 or 2 lemon wedges for serving

Kosher salt and freshly ground black pepper

6 medium leeks (about 3 pounds total)

1 cup freshly grated Parmigiano-Reggiano cheese (about 2 ounces)

Heat the oven to 425°F, with a rack in the middle.

Whisk the oil, herbs, Dijon, lemon zest and juice, ¼ teaspoon salt, and ⅛ teaspoon pepper in a bowl.

Trim the roots and dark green parts from the leeks and discard (or save to use for making stock). Halve the leeks lengthwise, rinse well, and pat dry, then arrange cut side up on a baking sheet. Spoon the oil mixture over the top, then rub it between the leaves. Turn the leeks cut side down and roast until softened and golden on the cut sides, 25 to 30 minutes.

Turn the leeks cut side up, sprinkle with the Parmesan, and continue roasting until the cheese is melted, 3 to 5 minutes more. Transfer the leeks to a platter, top with fresh herbs, season with pepper, and squeeze lemon over them. Serve hot or warm.

Celery with LEMON + Anchovy Butter

So often celery languishes in the veg drawer until its snappy stalks wilt and wither. Turns out all it needs are a couple of friends from your collection of pantry and fridge basics, and you get a dinner party-worthy hero you didn't even know existed. **SERVES 4**

2 tablespoons unsalted butter

2 tablespoons extra-virgin olive oil

1 tablespoon finely chopped anchovy fillets

¼ teaspoon red pepper flakes

1 large bunch celery (about 1¾ pounds), stalks separated cut on the bias into ¼-inch-thick pieces (reserve the leaves)

1 tablespoon grated lemon zest

Kosher salt and freshly ground black pepper

1 tablespoon fresh lemon juice, plus a big lemon wedge for serving

Flaky sea salt, such as Maldon (optional)

Heat the butter, oil, anchovies, and red pepper flakes in a large skillet over medium-high heat until the butter is melted. Add the celery and lemon zest, season with salt and pepper, and cook, stirring frequently, until the celery is crisp-tender, 3 to 5 minutes. Stir in the lemon juice and cook for 1 minute more.

Transfer to a platter, scraping all the good pan bits over the top. Sprinkle with the celery leaves, if using, then give it all a squeeze of lemon juice and a sprinkle of flaky salt, if desired, and serve.

Baked ZUCCHINI

with Cheesy Garlic Bread Crumbs

Melty underneath and crunchy on top, these tasty baked zucchini were inspired by the ones that my friend Ben Levine's mom, Lisa, makes in the summer when we grill outdoors. If you like, you can cook them ahead and let them come to room temp, then give them a quick blast in the oven to warm them just before serving. **SERVES 4**

¼ cup plus 2 table-spoons extra-virgin olive oil

2½ pounds zucchini or yellow summer squash, halved lengthwise

Kosher salt and freshly ground black pepper

1 cup panko (Japanese bread crumbs)

½ cup grated Parmigiano-Reggiano cheese

¼ cup chopped fresh flat-leaf parsley (optional, but I love)

¼ teaspoon red pepper flakes

2 garlic cloves, grated or minced

Heat the oven to 400°F.

Brush a baking sheet with 1 tablespoon of the oil. Arrange the zucchini cut side up on the baking sheet. Brush with 1 more tablespoon of the oil and season with ½ teaspoon salt and ¼ teaspoon black pepper.

Put the panko, Parmesan, parsley, if using, red pepper flakes, ½ teaspoon salt, and ¼ teaspoon black pepper in a bowl and add the garlic. Using your fingers, work the garlic into the bread crumbs until evenly combined. Drizzle the remaining ¼ cup oil over the bread crumbs and toss to coat.

Top the zucchini with the bread crumbs and bake until the zuke is tender and the bread crumbs are golden brown, 35 to 40 minutes. Serve hot or warm.

Index